SURVIVAL KNIVES

SURVIVAL KNIVES

How to Choose and Use the Right Blade

JAMES MORGAN AYRES

SKYHORSE PUBLISHING

Skyhorse Publishing books may be purchased in bulk at special discounts for sales promotion, corporate gifts, fund-raising, or educational purposes. Special editions can also be created to specifications. For details, contact the Special Sales Department, Skyhorse Publishing, 307 West 36th Street, 11th Floor, New York, NY 10018 or info@skyhorsepublishing.com.

Skyhorse® and Skyhorse Publishing® are registered trademarks of Skyhorse Publishing, Inc.®, a Delaware corporation.

Visit our website at www.skyhorsepublishing.com.

10 9 8 7 6 5 4 3 2

Library of Congress Cataloging-in-Publication Data is available on file.

Cover design by Tom Lau
Cover photo credit: James Morgan Ayres

Print ISBN: 978-1-5107-2842-4
Ebook ISBN: 978-1-5107-2843-1

Printed in China

CONTENTS

INTRODUCTION

*I*t might seem excessive to devote an entire book to a simple tool, but there is more to the survival knife and its uses than is immediately apparent. A survival knife could save your life. And so, it deserves our attention.

All the following events took place within the past few years; many were reported in the media:

- On 9/11, a young woman was inside a shipping container in Manhattan taking inventory when the explosions at the World Trade Center flipped the container onto its side, breaking her arm and trapping her. No one heard her cries for help for hours. She was growing weak and in much pain when a firefighter leaving the scene heard her. He had no tools with him other than his pocketknife, which happened to be a "tactical folder," a strong folding knife with certain attributes I will detail later in this book. Using a chunk of broken concrete, he pounded the blade of his knife through the steel-walled container, cut an opening, freed the woman, and got her medical attention.
- A windsurfer trying to windsurf across the Red Sea was stranded when the wind died. He was attacked by a pack of sharks. His only defense: his knife. He spent the night stabbing the sharks in the nose, eyes, and gills as they tried to pull him from his sailboard. His rescue came at dawn. Without his knife he wouldn't have survived the night.
- A businessman was having lunch with an associate in a revolving restaurant on top of a high-rise building in Manila when fire broke out in the kitchen and quickly spread into the dining room and throughout the top floor. As panic broke out, with people running in circles and screaming, and knowing that the elevators would be frozen, this man ushered his companion to the fire stairs. When he reached the bottom floor he discovered that it was chained and locked, which was common in Manila due to frequent theft. By now a mob of panicked diners filled the staircase behind him, shoving, yelling, trampling. He turned to the crowd and in a commanding voice told them to "Stop!" and that he would get everyone out safely. He then used his knife to cut a wedge-shaped hole in the steel fire door. Everyone got out safely.
- On a summer day in the Midwest, a powerful tornado came up quickly, as they often do, and overturned a truck, dropping it upside down in a ditch, crushing the cab and windshield. The doors wouldn't open and the driver was trapped. The gas tank ruptured and fuel rapidly pooled in the cab. The driver, who was wearing a small belt knife, used his knife to cut an opening in the rear of the cab and climb to safety.
- A young couple was hiking on a trail at the edge of the desert a few miles from Los Angeles when they saw a cool stream running in a concrete channel. Hot and parched, the young man stripped to his shorts and jumped in, not knowing that the stream was actually the California Aqueduct. Upstream, the sluice gates had been opened and a wall of icy snow-melt water soon engulfed him. He hung onto an irregularity in the concrete but couldn't get a strong hold to pull himself out. He went into thermal shock, his muscles cramping

and spasming, his fingers growing numb. He called to his wife, telling her to slide his knife to him. She did. He wedged the knife into a crack and used it as a pivot point to pull himself to safety.

- During the earthquake in Haiti, a young backpacker was trapped in her hostel when the building collapsed. She used her pocketknife to dig her way to a small opening, where rescuers could hear her calls for help. She was saved with only a few bruises and scratches.

- Most of us have heard the story of Aron Ralston, an outdoorsman whose arm was trapped under a boulder in a canyon deep in a wilderness area in Utah. After being trapped for over five days, he amputated his own arm with the blade of a multitool, and walked to safety.

- A honeymoon couple's canoe overturned during an unexpected summer storm on Lake Michigan. Their canoe and all supplies were swept away. They swam through high waves to shore and climbed from the water, soaking wet, miles from help with no tent, sleeping bags, or food. Both were experienced outdoors people and had knives on their belts and spark rods in their pockets. Within an hour they had a fire going, had built a snug shelter, and their clothing was drying.

- A salesman was tired after a long day at work and not paying much attention to his surroundings. While parking his car he was startled to see a zombie charging from the shadows. He quickly reached for his survival knife and . . . Okay, that didn't really happen, just checking to see if you're awake.

These people saved their own lives, or those of others, with the aid of man's oldest and most versatile and portable tool—the knife. A Hooligan Tool (used by firefighters) would be better for digging out from the rubble of a collapsed building. The Jaws of Life, used by rescue people, would be more efficient to extract a person from a wrecked car. A strong rope would be a better tool for climbing from icy water. In a forest, an ax will get you firewood and shelter with less effort. The thing is, you aren't likely to have any of those tools at hand in an emergency. On the other hand, you can have a survival knife with you at all times. Read this book and you will learn how to choose a good survival knife and how to use one. Doing so might save your life.

The working model for the methods described in this book is that you have only your knife and the contents of your pockets to survive, no survival kit, ready bag, or bug-out bag. Often survival situations develop when, and sometimes because, you have no gear except what's on your person. In military terminology this is "first-line gear." We will only touch lightly on other first-line gear in this book and keep the focus on the knife and its uses. One of my other books, *Essential Survival Gear*, goes into detail on first-, second-, third-, and fourth-line gear, and how to select and most effectively use such equipment.

In this book we will examine that most fundamental and essential tool, the knife, the ways in which purpose-built survival knives differ from other knives, and why the knife is so important a tool. Most importantly, we will learn how to use the knife to aid survival in extreme situations, and why the survival knife should be used as an everyday tool, rather than tucked away for a contingent emergency.

The use of a knife to save your life is a topic not well covered in other books. Do you know the best way to use your survival knife to escape a burning building, or a building collapsed by an earthquake? You may have seen illustrations of how to make primitive hunting weapons, such as bows and spears, but do you know how to successfully hunt with such weapons? Mere possession of a knife, even a specialized survival knife, and the skill to make, say, a primitive bow, does not ensure your survival or that of your loved ones. Read this book, practice the skills herein, and become a survivor.

Stories and Structure

In this book I will discuss and demonstrate a range of survival knives, and provide instruction on their use. This book, however, is not structured as a dry field manual. In general, field manuals are useful as references and as teaching aids in classes. They are less useful as self-contained texts without a teacher, or without having previously taken classes on the topic. From teaching many classes, and from having students tell me years after a class that they remembered a story I had told to illustrate a point, I've found that people remember stories long after dry facts are forgotten, and that a description of gear doesn't do much to inform or teach.

Like my students, I too recall stories told to me decades ago by childhood mentors and other teachers. Much of what we think of today as survival skills were simply life skills for our grandparents, or perhaps, great grandparents, and were passed on to me, and others of my generation, as stories. That tradition, that person-to-person chain of knowledge, has, due to our ever-more-urban society, been broken. It is my intention to mend that break in whatever small way I can.

It's an old tradition, storytelling. All preliterate societies used stories to pass on information. The advent of writing reinforced the practice. So, in this book I'll tell some stories, hopefully engaging ones, and relate some personal experiences and practices to illustrate the uses of survival knives, and to provide some practical examples of survival behavior. I've also found that the process of extracting the lesson from the story aids in absorbing and retaining the lesson, partially because the reader puts himself in the place of the person in the story. Each of these stories teaches lessons. After reading each story, ask yourself what lesson the story taught. Absorb the lessons and learn how to survive in an urban disaster zone or wilderness area, or, really, anyplace on our planet, with only a knife.

*NOTE: This is my third book in a series on survival. The first two were *The Tao of Survival* and *Essential Survival Gear*. Future books to come will address survival in the broad sense, which includes surviving illness, urban disturbances, natural disasters, and the vicissitudes of daily life, rather than in the narrow sense of surviving being lost in wilderness.

In this book there is a small amount of material carried over from *The Tactical Knife* (Skyhorse, 2014). Basic cuts and sharpening and a few tips are foundational and need to be included and I saw no point in rewriting these instructions. I also include fire-making instructions that are in *The Tao of Survival* and *Essential Survival Gear*. I once saw a fifteen-year old boy die of hypothermia when he got lost during a weekend snowboarding outing. He died because he didn't know how to make fire. This experience affected me profoundly and led to my offering free classes for young people in fire-making and basic survival skills—an offer that is still open. I've witnessed many others who suffered greatly, and also know of others who have died from lack of this skill. Fire-making is a critical lifesaving skill, and a lost art for the general population. Therefore, I will most likely in the future include fire-making instructions in every book I write, including novels.

Chapter One

Defining the Survival Knife

The Knife You Have with You

The most frequent question regarding survival knives is, "What is the best survival knife?" There's an old saying that the best survival knife is the one you have with you when you need to survive. Although this begs the question of what features the ideal survival knife should have, there is a large measure of wisdom in that saying, and many stories that illustrate this point.

In today's mobile and fast-moving world, anyone can find him or herself in a survival situation at any time and any place. Six of the eight instances cited in the introduction to this book took place in urban or fringe areas. There are many other occurrences in which a knife enabled a person to survive a life-threatening event in areas that were not wilderness.

At a social gathering in Washington D.C., I met a young man who worked for a humanitarian NGO (nongovernmental organization) who told me he had been kidnapped by a militia group, basically a bunch of teenagers stoned on *khat* (a stimulant) and carrying AKs, while working in Somalia. They took him to a war-damaged building in Mogadishu and locked him into a closet, presumably, he thought, to await the arrival of their commander. He knew of this group and of the common practice of kidnapping Westerners in Somalia. Based on what had happened to others, he figured he would be held for an extended period while his ransom was being negotiated. He did not

want to wait through a dangerous captivity, one that could turn violent at any time, and was concerned that his kidnappers would ask for more money than his organization, friends, and family could raise. He decided to try to escape.

During a long night, while the guard outside the closet door slept deep in drugged sleep and his other captors had wandered off, he dug his way through a plaster wall with his pocketknife, an ordinary Swiss Army knife with a few tools. He used the main blade and screwdriver blades to work through the plaster, cut the wire underneath, and whittle through the wooden lath. Working slowly and quietly he made a small hole in the wall, and while his guard continued to sleep, crawled through the hole, climbed out of a window, and made his way to a secure area. He showed me the beat up, blunted, and chipped SAK he carried in his pocket and told me he intended to buy another one with a locking blade. This one had closed on his fingers and cut him when he was stabbing and prying through the wall. He planned to frame this one.

Recently a friend I correspond with traveled the length of Africa on local transportation: buses, freight trucks, and private vehicles, often camping out or staying in village homes and hostels. He wrote me that on two separate occasions he avoided robbery, and possibly worse, by small groups of men with machetes who demanded his money and rucksack, and that he go with them. He responded both times by drawing his six-inch bladed knife from his waistband under his shirt, showing no fear, and responding with aggressive body language and telling them they were going to get hurt more than he was if they didn't leave him alone. In both instances they retreated, most likely in search of someone easier to victimize. He wrote that he had used his knife every day for everything from food preparation and camping chores, to helping to butcher a slaughtered cow at a village festival. He was sure that if he had not had his knife, the tool he used daily, that the attempted robberies would not have turned out as they did.

Bud Nealy, a custom knifemaker, relates the story of one of his customers who used one of Nealy's small fixed-blade knives to cut an escape hatch through the roof of a car that had plunged into an icy lake in Finland. A neighbor told me he once went to visit a friend whose wife had recently left him and found that his friend had hanged himself in his garage. My neighbor quickly cut him down with his pocketknife, applied CPR, and called the paramedics. His friend survived and later thanked him for saving his life. I read in the news last year about a woman skiing off piste in Romania who became lost and was forced to spend a winter night alone in the mountains. When the searchers found her the next day, she was sitting comfortably by a fire she had built with the aid of her pocketknife and a butane lighter.

The stories are many, and these events continue to happen. I have a few of those stories myself: I was that businessman who had to cut through a steel fire door to escape a burning high rise. At the age of ten I fell into an icy river far from home. A Boy Scout knife and knowing how to make fire saved me from freezing to death. Those stories I've related in detail in *The Tactical Knife* and *Essential Survival Gear*. There

are other stories I'll tell in this book. These stories, mine and others, illustrate the reality that a knife can aid survival in circumstances none can foresee, that those circumstances do not always happen in wilderness, and that the knife that is used in survival situations is the knife the person had with them—purpose designed or not, fixed blade or folder.

In urban and fringe areas, in the event of an earthquake or other disaster, you might have to cut and rip through wood, wire, and stucco and grind through concrete. You might have to cut though an auto body or a shipping container. You might have to make shelter from debris such as sheet metal and plastic roofing. That being so, it is worthwhile to select a knife that is bettered suited to urban survival than one that is not, as the young NGO worker said he intended to do. Not that an SAK with a locking blade is the best possible urban or hard-use survival knife, but it is better than one without a locking blade and it did fit his particular circumstances. A small but sturdy fixed blade would have better served him to rip through a wall. But his organization did not allow their workers to have fixed blades, and he thought his captors might have found a fixed blade and taken it from him. They didn't find his SAK and so he decided to continue with what had worked for him in the past.

A light wood carving knife, such as a basic Mora, an inexpensive Swedish-made knife popular with bushcraft enthusiasts, might be all you need in the woods, and that same knife *might* do to dig your way out of a collapsed building—if you know how, a skill I cover later in this book. Like the fellow who was kidnapped, you might be able cut your way through a wall with a SAK. But, a sturdy fixed blade, even a

▲ SAK Soldier's Knife.

▲ Chris Reeve Sebenza.

▲ Fällkniven F1.

small one, makes a better urban survival tool. It will allow you to rip, tear, gouge, hack, and pry through plaster and lath walls, concrete block, brick walls, wood, bamboo, sheet-metal walls, aircraft skins, auto bodies, steel fire doors, or any door, really. You can also use it as a lever to move broken stone and concrete, smash out the window of an overturned bus or train, and all in all serve as an escape or rescue device and urban destructo tool. This category of knife—sturdy fixed blades with blades of about four inches—are what I think of as "traveler's knives." Small enough for discrete daily urban carry, they raise no eyebrows in most field conditions, will pass most customs inspections, and function well as all-around utility knives. Traveler's knife, tactical folder, SAK, whatever knife you have with you when the moment comes—that will be your survival knife.

The Purpose-Designed Survival Knife

The modern concept of a purpose-designed survival knife dates from World War Two and the Cold War. Obviously, before that time knives were used for survival functions. But usually, in wilderness travel, war, or in a home environment, other tools and or weapons were available. In effect, the knife was part of a tool kit. That being so, knives from earlier periods were for the most part optimized for their primary function, cutting, with little thought given to other qualities—the exception being knives and short swords designed as weapons. In such use, a broken blade could be fatal. And so, edged weapons were designed with strength and cutting ability as coequal functions.

World War Two was different than all preceding wars in that it was global and fast moving, a war of fire and movement. Front lines shifted quickly, mechanized transport and armor, aircraft, and ships transported troops to locations far from their friendly bases. As a result, soldiers were often cut off from support and had to rely on their training and whatever tools and weapons they had on their person to survive until they could rejoin their main forces. In addition, new units were formed, commandos and special operations groups that operated fully self-contained in hostile territory and had to be equipped to survive with no support, possibly for extended periods. Aviators were a special class in that they commonly flew over enemy lines and, if shot down or otherwise grounded, were on their own until they could be rescued or escape.

In 1942, the Marine Corps, which fought throughout the Pacific Theatre on many isolated islands, adapted the KA-BAR, a relatively lightweight seven-inch bladed design with a clip point based on the Bowie knife. This knife was effective as a weapon and all-around utility and survival knife. Its blade was made of high carbon steel, took a sharp edge, and was reasonably tough and long enough to reach viral organs in close combat. The KA-BAR's non-slip

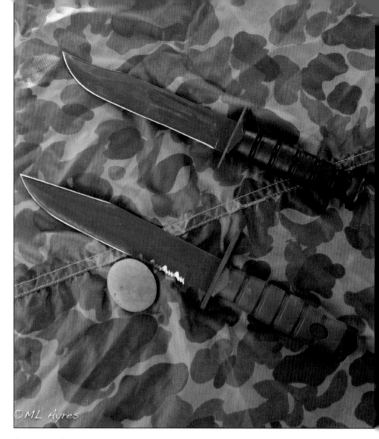

▲ KA-BAR knives.

stacked leather handle provided a secure grip even when wet or slippery. The steel pommel that was useful for pounding test stakes also functioned as an impact weapon. The KA-BAR proved its value in hand-to-hand fights to the death, and during years of living under primitive conditions proved critical to the survival of many Marines who were cut off and isolated for periods. The KA-BAR, in various finishes, is still in production today, over sixty years after its introduction, a testament to its usefulness.

Army troops, well aware of the value of the KA-BAR, had no such knife issued to them and had to make do with issued bayonets, which were tempered soft to resist impact and unable to take a razor edge. As a result, whenever possible, many soldiers obtained KA-BARs from Marines, in trade or by outright purchase. Others bought their own knives from civilian sources. Paratroopers, who were dropped behind enemy lines as a matter of course,

▲ Randall Model 1.

and other special operations units that operated far from support, had specialized knives. American paratroopers in particular favored Randall knives. But Randall knives were relatively expensive and beyond the means of many soldiers. Some soldiers who had been hunters and had backcountry and wilderness experience brought various kitchen or hunting knives to war. Some of those worked well, some failed in use.

The Cold War and its particular dynamics intensified the need for survival knives. During these years, from the end of World War Two until the fall of the Berlin Wall in 1989, thousands of covert operators and clandestine agents in dozens of undeclared and low conflict zones around the world had need of survival knives, as did military aviators, who needed smaller knives than ground troops due to the space limitations of their cockpits. But the aviator's knives had to be equally functional, sturdy, and sharp.

The Aviator's Survival Knife in a number of different configurations was designed specifically to fill this need, and was adapted by the military for Army, Navy, and Air Force pilots and crew members who wore it attached to their survival vests. This knife, in various editions, is still used today in air crew survival training, and still worn by many military pilots

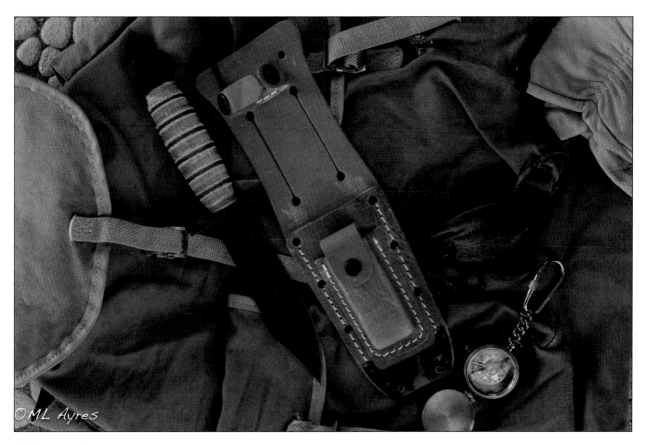

▲ Pilot Survivor by Ontario Knives.

when flying. Its specific features—a steel pommel suitable for smashing through an aircraft window, saw teeth on the spine for cutting through the skin of an aircraft and making notches in wood for traps, and a five-inch blade of high carbon steel—were designed to allow air crews to exit damaged aircraft and carry a small amount of other gear to survive on land or at sea. This knife has been used to good effect by generations of military aviators. In one recorded incident during the Vietnam War, a pilot who had parachuted to earth after his plane was shot down was attacked by a machete wielding Vietnamese. The pilot defended himself and dispatched his attacker with his Aviator's Survival Knife.

By the middle to late sixties, with armed conflicts between the superpowers and their client states continuing in Southeast Asia, Latin America, and Africa, and with low-intensity conflicts virtually everywhere around the world, the need for purpose-designed-and-built survival knives was well understood by the military and paramilitary organizations, and by many civilians who went into harm's way. A civilian market made up of adventurers, explorers, and world travelers also emerged. Cutlery companies responded to these needs and began making specialty survival knives in many varieties. During the seventies and eighties the civilian market for the purpose-designed survival knife exploded, resulting in new developments such as the "tactical folder," which in essence redefined the parameters of folding knives. New blade steels have been brought to the market. Some of them will hold a sharp edge as well as a well-tempered basic carbon steel, if made by a knifemaker who knows how to handle these new steels. Some of these steels also require a much longer time to sharpen.

Today we have a large selection of purpose-designed survival knives to choose from. Some of them fulfill the needs of a survivor very well. Others, which are designed for the market by those who have no actual survival experience or understanding of what is needed in survival knives, do not work well at all.

▲ Mykel Hawke's Peregrine, Spartan Harsey Difensa fixed blade, TOPS Zero Dark 30.

Chapter Two

Selecting Your Survival Knife

We return to the question, what is the best survival knife? The real question is this: What is the best survival knife for you and your circumstances? Many associate the need for a survival knife with wilderness use. However, a survival situation can arise anytime and anyplace, as we saw in the instances recounted in the introduction to this book, and as we see in the daily news.

The Rambo knife, with its nine-inch blade, saw-tooth back, and hollow handle, might be just the thing when you're lost in the woods. But will you have it with you? A well-designed-and-made large knife with a nine- to ten-inch blade will do almost everything better and faster than a small knife can do, but few of us live in circumstances where we can, or would choose to, carry such a big knife on our person. For most of us such knives are carried in a pack or bag and should be thought of as secondary knives rather than primary survival knives.

You might want to do as most experienced survival instructors do and carry a conveniently sized knife appropriate to your daily life on your person and a larger blade in your bag, making adjustments according to your activity and location. A small folder with a reliable lock on your person and a four-inch fixed blade in your daypack might be suitable for a day hike or some fishing near home, or a trip around the world. A medium-sized fixed blade on your belt and a small machete in your rucksack would, of course, be better choices for an extended trip in a tropical rainforest.

Following are some general categories of knives, by size. There is overlap from one category to another. For example, at the upper end of the "Medium" category we have the seven-inch bladed KA-BAR and at the lower end the Pilot's Survival Knife. Actually, there is a continuum from small knife to big knife, but these divisions are useful to help us to analyze functions and make choices. The comments in this section are of a general nature and deal with functionality according to knife size. I'll go into more detail regarding individual knives in another section of this book.

Choppers

Knives with blades over ten inches in length, such as machetes, parangs, goloks, bolos, and so on, are vitally important in the jungle and very useful elsewhere. With one you can make a shelter and primitive tools, open coconuts, and in general do many things much faster than with smaller blades. With this size blade you can simply slash through a two-inch-thick sapling with one stroke, whereas you might spend three to five minutes to take down the same size sapling with a small knife and a baton. Multiply this by, say, twenty saplings you might need for a shelter framework and we're looking at a considerable difference in time and calories expended to do the job.

With a minimum of instruction, these big blades are safer to use than a hatchet. The cutting edge is much longer than the hatchet's and the modestly skilled person is less likely to miss their target and overswing, perhaps resulting in an injury. Over the years I have seen many more students at military and civilian survival schools injured by hatchet use than by machete use.

People who live close to the earth carry and use these big blades on a daily basis. The Central and South American machete, S.E. Asian parangs, goloks and bolos, the Nepalese kukri, the African panga—all are daily tools of choice for the people of those areas for bush work, agriculture, and all-around use. They are also fearsome weapons.

These choppers are not at all convenient to carry unless you're actually in the bush, in which case you'll do well to keep one close to hand at all times. I prefer big blades over hatchets for all areas, and when in wilderness often

▲ Condor Golok, Condor Barong, Tramontina Machete.

carry a twelve-inch machete in my rucksack, as do many survival instructors, experienced outdoors people, military personnel, and bush travelers in lesser developed nations.

Large Fixed-Blade Knives

Big knives, with seven- to ten-inch blades, do not chop as well as the machetes and parangs but are more versatile than any chopper. They are also more efficient for many, perhaps most, wilderness tasks than medium and small knives. With a minimum of instruction and experience, and with, say, a well-designed nine-inch bladed Bowie, a survivor can do everything from skinning a mouse to quickly opening up a dead log to get at the dry wood inside.

The frontiersmen and hunters who opened up the Northwest and ranged through deep uncharted wilderness on foot and with only what they could carry without exception carried and used the big knife as their all-purpose tool and weapon. The Lapland Leku, with a blade in the seven- to nine-inch range, is still today the all-purpose cutting tool of virtually every trapper, hunter, herder, and outdoors person around the Arctic Circle, from Finland to Siberia and from Mongolia to China.

▲ Browning Model 580 Crowell/Barker design, Condor Hudson Bay, Condor Matagi, CRKT Ken Onion design, Defender, Spyderco Forester FB 16P Jerry Hossom design—a selection of well-proven big knives.

▲ AG Russell's Bowie cuts through one-inch hanging hemp with ease.

Ask any professional chef or butcher what knife he or she would choose if only one knife were available. The chef will select a nine- or ten-inch chef's knife, the butcher a ten-inch breaker. When you have a lot of work to do, the big knife shines. After a week of bush work, more than one of my students has selected a well-designed Bowie or a Leku as an all-around wilderness blade.

With a proper sheath, a big knife is far more convenient to carry than a chopper. However, with few exceptions the big knife is too big to carry on your person unless you are actually in the wilderness. Like the smaller machetes, these knives mostly live in rucksacks until their owners step off the pavement.

Medium-Sized Fixed-Blade Knives

Medium-sized knives, with five- to seven-inch blades, are efficient for most critical survival functions and are a good compromise in carry convenience between the big blade and small utility knives. There is a considerable difference in performance between, say, the seven-inch bladed KA-BAR, which is used by Marines and is at the upper edge of this category, and the five-inch bladed Pilot's Survival Knife, which is at the bottom. But for our purposes, both fit into this category.

The medium-sized knife is not as good a chopper as the big knife; some, depending on balance, weight, and grind, will not chop at all and are better batoned. Depending on the user and the individual knife, the medium-size knife can be less handy for small tasks than a four-inch utility or "bushcraft" knife. Such smaller blades in the four-inch range might be somewhat handier for fine woodworking but lose out to the medium-sized blade for such wilderness tasks as *quickly* making a survival shelter and splitting

wet wood to get to the dry wood inside, and for urban tasks such as digging out from a collapsed building.

A properly designed and executed six-inch blade can do light chopping and in the right hands is as efficient as any "bushcraft" knife for small woodwork. I sometimes think of the medium-sized blade as the Volkswagen camper of survival knives—it does everything reasonably well and is small enough to park most anywhere. In many ways the properly designed and constructed medium-sized knife is closest to the ideal of the "all-around survival knife."

©ML Ayres

▲ Daniel Winkler's belt knife comes in handy for removing the spines from a palm frond to be used as a shade in the heat.

Many military survival experts agree that the KA-BAR, with its longer blade, is the better last-ditch weapon and all-around utility and survival knife for the ground soldier. The Pilot's Survival Knife, with its five-inch blade, was designed to be big enough and strong enough to cut through the skin of an aircraft (so the user can escape from a downed plane), function as an all-around survival tool and emergency self-defense weapon, yet be small enough to carry on a pilot's survival vest and in the close quarters of an aircraft. Both knives have fulfilled their functions for more than fifty years.

Despite this, the medium-sized knife is still too large for daily carry for many civilians, certainly for most urbanites. Perhaps it is the "ideal all-around survival knife," but if it's too large for you to carry daily, it's not the optimal choice for your primary survival knife.

Small Fixed-Blade Knives

Straddling categories, the well-designed and executed four- to five-inch fixed blade is possibly the best choice for many, possibly most, people as an all-around fixed blade survival knife. It's big enough to do hard work and small enough to carry at all times, or at least most of the time. These smaller fixed blades, with blades around four inches in length, are good all-around utility knives. Although not as efficient as the medium-sized knife, they will serve well for survival functions, if well designed and made, and if the user knows what he's doing.

Chopping with a small knife is futile. The leverage provided by a longer blade is absent, as is the weight of a larger knife. Rather than ineffectively hacking at a log to split off thin slivers with a four-inch blade, use a baton. The small blade will not allow the deep slicing cuts

you would use to break down, say, a deer carcass. But by making shallower slices and more of them, you can accomplish the same task. Getting through a concrete block wall is easier with a long-bladed knife because you can reach deep into the cracks where mortar holds the blocks together. But with patience and a strong small knife, you can indeed work your way through such a wall.

"Bushcraft" knives, characterized by four-inch blades and "Scandi" grinds, are currently popular, and many highly skilled survival instructors whose focus is on wilderness survival choose them as all an-around daily use and survival knife. Bushcraft knives vary considerably. Some are lightly constructed and have thin blades that are good slicers but subject to bending under hard use. Others are quite stout and function well as small survival knives for urban as well as wilderness conditions. Still other small fixed blades are purpose-designed survival knives, their size parameters set by available space and ease of carry, and work very well for survival functions as well as being suited for everyday use.

Knives in this category are, generally speaking—depending on sheath and carry method—more convenient to carry than larger knives. Therein lies the small fixed blade's most important quality. For many, small fixed blades qualify as the "with you" knife. Often the key to convenient carry is the sheath. Most manufacturers provide sheaths that are reasonably well suited for bush carry. Those same sheaths may not be comfortable if you are climbing in and out of vehicles and may get caught in door jams or other machinery. Nor do many sheaths provide for discreet carry, which may be desirable. With a proper sheath, the small fixed

▲ Condor Bushcraft making shavings for a fire. Photo credit: Justin Ayres.

blade can be as easy to carry as a folder while being far stronger. I think of small fixed blades as "traveler's knives" in that they are easy to tote, acceptable almost everywhere, and are the most versatile of knives. In many ways the small fixed-blade survival knife—the Fällkniven F1 as an example that has set a standard over two decades—has for many become *the* survival knife of the twenty-first century.

Tiny Knives

Both fixed blades and folders with blades less than three inches in length, some even less than two inches, are also useful in survival situations. These small knives are not optimal, but they might be more acceptable according to local norms, or allow discrete carry, and therefore may be the knife you have with you. You can accomplish many of the same tasks with a small knife that you can accomplish with a large one, if you use proper technique, and if you have enough time. In any case, they serve as good second or even third knives, and are so unobtrusive that there's really no reason not to have one.

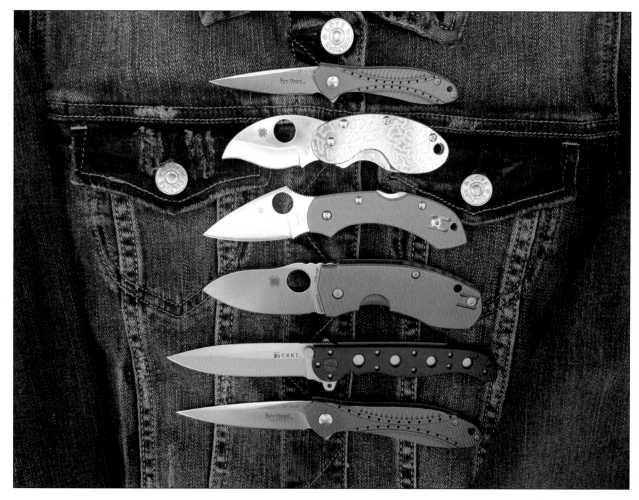

▲ A collection of tiny knives.

◄ A Fred Perrin (a well-known French knife maker) LaGriffe splitting a feather for fletching an arrow.

©ML Ayres

Military/Combat/Survival Knives

Many soldiers deployed in combat zones need robust knives that can serve as daily-use, all-purpose tools, emergency survival tools, and weapons of last resort. Due to the nature of conventional warfare today, and to the areas in which today's wars are being fought, this is, perhaps, less true today than in previous conflicts. However, many combat troops prefer to have the same kind of knife previous generations carried to war. A war knife typically has a blade of about seven inches, which is the length that was determined by military research in World War II to be the minimum required to reach an enemy's vital organs through winter clothing. Blades are usually about a quarter inch thick, usually have clip points, often a non-reflective finish, and in general are exceptionally strong. A non-slip handle is standard, as is a full tang, either slab or rat tail. Due to their size and general appearance, which will alarm some people, these blades may not be the best choice for the civilian seeking a survival knife. But they will certainly function in that role.

Many soldiers in today's conflict zones have elected to carry a small fixed blade instead of, or in addition to, a war knife. The accompanying photos show some of these in use.

▲ Spartan Phrike carried on load-bearing equipment. Photo credit: Spartan Knives.

Small Military Fixed Blade Knives

▲ Spartan Enyo carried on hip of soldier. Photo credit: Spartan Knives.

Large Military Fixed-Blade Knives

▲ CRKT Elishewitz and Becker Knife & Tool breaking through a wall.

Folding Survival Knives

A solid well-made folder, a "tactical folder" in current terminology, can accomplish far more than many survival experts would have us believe. It is important to know what can be accomplished with a folding knife, because the most commonly carried knife is the folder, which results in it becoming the most commonly used survival knife in the world.

Due to their construction, folders were once considered fit only for light work. That was more or less true, my Boy Scout knife notwithstanding. That perception of folders began to change about thirty years ago when Al Mar and Colonel James "Nick" Rowe designed the SERE (Survival Evasion Resistance and Escape) folding knife. Al Mar was an extraordinarily talented knife designer and a former Special Forces (Green Beret) soldier. Colonel Rowe was also a Special Forces soldier, a POW in Vietnam, the founder of the US Military SERE school, and developer of the doctrine now taught to all high-risk military personal, including Special Forces.

Colonel Rowe initially identified the need for the SERE folder. He knew that soldiers have a tendency to dump their load-bearing gear when it's not needed. Military fixed blades are usually carried on load-bearing gear, along with many other items vital to the soldier's mission. When this gear is not worn, which is much of the time, the solider lacks a critically needed survival tool and emergency weapon. Colonel Rowe conceived the concept for a survival knife that would be smaller and easier to carry than any fixed blade, yet robust enough for survival requirements, and which would be carried on the soldier's belt or in one of his pockets rather than on load-bearing gear.

His collaboration with Al Mar resulted in the first purpose-designed folding survival knife. Colonel Rowe's vision proved prophetic. Today, due to the obvious value of the SERE and to further development of the concept by others, virtually every combat soldier and millions of civilians carry folders that are conceptual descendants of the SERE.

Additional innovations in folder design occurred in the eighties. Sal Glesser, the founder of Spyderco, introduced the pocket clip and the hole in the blade that allowed for one-hand opening. Other one-handed opening devices such as blade studs soon followed. Michael Walker, an American custom knife maker, reintroduced and modified the liner lock, which led to further innovations in locking systems. Over time, many folding knives were developed that are now called "tactical folders." Some tactical folders are suitable for use as survival knives, if they have the following features:

- Robust construction, especially at the joint, because the folding survival knife may be required for extreme tasks such as deconstructing a wall or cutting through a shipping container.
- Strong and reliable lock, because a knife blade closing on the user's finger could be disabling and in survival conditions lead to infection and possible loss of fingers.
- One-hand opening because the user may only have one hand available due to injury or to having the other hand occupied.
- A pocket clip because it secures the folder from loss and makes it readily available.

A well-designed and executed folder with these features and with a three-and one-half to four- and one-half-inch blade has, for many, replaced the small fixed blade. Such a folder conveniently fulfills the first requirement of a survival knife—have it with you—and can be relied on as long as you work within its limits and don't do anything that would cause it to fold. Prying on the lateral plane of the blade puts so much pressure on the joint that it could lead to failure. Improper batoning technique can cause a lock to fail. Stabbing into a hard material, such as oak, and twisting can also lead to lock failure, and might break the tip of your blade—any blade, fixed or folder. To ensure reliability in a survival folder, choose one from a top-quality manufacturer and keep the mechanism clean so that lint or other pocket debris, or miscellaneous materials (splinters and so on), do not get into the locking mechanism. Keeping these cautions in mind, and because the folder excels in the "with you" factor, using a top-quality folder with the necessary features as an everyday survival knife is a workable option.

I have trained many young people in basic wilderness survival methods using as the only knives that I think of as "survival folders." I was

▲ Top to bottom: Mykel Hawke Harrier, Cold Steel Voyager, Pohl Force Alpha 2, Spyderco Military, CRKT Carson Design M21.

motivated to do this after witnessing a teenage boy die for want of a little basic knowledge, a knife, and a fire starter. He had been snow-boarding off piste and got lost. The SAR team found him after he had spent three nights out in winter mountain weather with only his inadequate clothing (a topic I address in *Essential Survival Gear*) and no survival gear at all, not even a butane lighter. The team was too late to save him from fatal hypothermia. He was never more than a mile from the ski lodge.

I watched the light fade from his eyes and felt his fear as he faced the unknown. I saw the anguish and despair on the faces of his

▲ Butane lighter and stainless-steel waterproof match case.

parents and felt their pain as he slipped away. I experienced the frustration and sorrow of the medical team that tried to save him. And at that moment I decided to do whatever I could do to pass on potentially lifesaving knowledge that was once part of most children's education but which has faded with the urbanization of our culture.

In response to this tragedy, and to learning that the majority of accidental wilderness deaths that occur in the US today are from hypothermia, I developed a one-day seminar and have offered it for years to any and all on a *pro bono* basis, with special focus on outreach to teenagers. In this seminar I teach elementary awareness and "don't get lost training," fire making, shelter building, signaling, and the importance of wearing proper clothing.

The only equipment used, other than proper clothing, is a top-quality survival folder, a butane lighter, and a small flint stick. I selected this equipment because young backpackers, skiers, snowboarders, climbers, and others who use the wilderness for recreation will not, due to peer pressure, social norms, or legal restrictions, carry a fixed blade. Nor will they carry any gear that their peers think isn't cool. A folder and a lighter can be tucked away out of sight and the flint stick goes on a key ring unobtrusively. This minimal gear does not get in the way of snowboarding, skiing, backpacking, rafting, or climbing, and draws little or no attention from others. Few of the kids, or adults, I have trained have any notion of equipment maintenance. So I selected folders with stainless blades that would hold their edge during much use, and butane lighters and sparkers because they require no maintenance. None of the folks I have trained has ever been lost or needed rescue, for which I

am thankful. Simple tools and a little knowledge can save lives.

These folding knives can save lives in other ways too. A Marine I correspond with was forced into mortal combat with a terrorist in Iraq when the only weapon he possessed was a tactical folder clipped to his uniform blouse. When I asked him why he used his folder instead of his KA-BAR, he told me his KA-BAR was attached to his web gear and, along with his carbine, not within reach. He said the folder was "right there when I needed it." He prevailed in his struggle due to having that blade, an event Colonel Rowe and Al Mar might have foreseen many years ago.

One disadvantage for survival purposes of some tactical folders is that they have very thin handles that are uncomfortable in extended hard use. This can be partially compensated for by, after opening the blade, wrapping the handle with cord or a handkerchief or both, or wearing gloves. Better yet, select a survival folder with a comfortable handle. That said, few folders of any kind have handles as comfortable for hard work as well-designed fixed blades. The best survival folders are not as strong or reliable as good-quality small fixed blades. But for most people, they fulfill the "with you" function better than any fixed blades.

Locks on Folding Knives

Given that the blade lock for a survival folder is of critical importance, we'll take a closer look at the most popular locks in use today. All of these locks engage automatically when the blade is opened.

The lockback uses a strong back spring with a lug, either straight or inclined, that snaps into a notch at the back of the blade. There are two variations: front and back releases.

▲ Four lockbacks: Cold Steel, Spyderco, Swiss Army, Pohl Force.

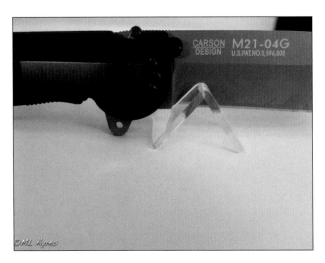

The liner lock utilizes a spring steel bar that swings into place and blocks the blade from closing by butting up to the blade tang.

◄ CRKT Carson Design M21, knife, liner lock with close-up of the safety.

The frame lock functions the same way as the liner lock but uses a portion of the frame as the locking bar.

▲ Chris Reeve's Sebenza, frame lock originator.

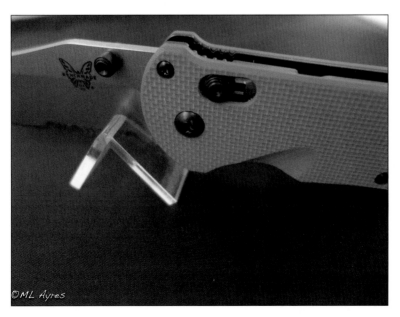

◄ Benchmade Axis lock.

All of the above locks are in common use by knifemakers, and all work well if properly executed.

The Axis Lock is proprietary to the Benchmade Knife Company and is an excellent design, both strong and reliable.

The Compression Lock is proprietary to Spyderco Knives and is also an excellent design, reliable and very strong.

©ML Ayres

▲ Close-up, compression lock, Spyderco Para-Military.

One other proprietary lock I have much experience with deserves mention. It is the Virobloc or twist lock of Opinel Knives. This lock is not automatically engaged when the blade is opened, nor is this knife designed to open with one hand. But with a bit of fiddling you can manage to open and engage the lock one handed.

More important than lock design is quality in manufacturing. Poorly made locking folders

are not to be relied upon and should not be selected for survival use. Lock failure can result in severe, possibly disabling, injury. Most high-quality locking folders are fairly expensive. With only a couple of exceptions, if you cannot afford a good-quality locking folder, you are better off selecting a good, inexpensive fixed blade.

One of those exceptions, the Opinel, is a very affordable folder with an exceptionally

▲ Standard Opinel with a ready-to-eat picnic.

comfortable handle, a blade that takes a ferocious edge, and a reliable lock. It is, however, a lightly made knife, suitable for woodcarving and general use, including light-duty wilderness use, but less useful for extreme urban use. Also, the Opinel lacks a clip, although one could be attached.

Non-locking Folders

Due to the stresses of survival situations and because you might be called upon to do unanticipated and extreme things with your survival knife, a reliable locking blade is virtually a requirement for a survival folder. However, if the need arises, you can make do with a slip joint, which is what my Boy Scout knife was. Many ordinary pocketknives are slip joints, which hold the blade in closed or open position with the back spring but which are not secure for hard use. Use these knives with caution. Everyone I've known who has used a slip joint for survival purposes has at some point cut themselves with it, including me.

▲ Turkish folding yatagan with sheep horn handle, carbon steel blade, convex ground.

Another type of non-locking folder is the friction folder, which holds the blade in place by the friction between the handles and the blade. In some examples there is an extended lever at the back of the blade that can be secured with the user's hand.

Multi-blade Folding Knives

Virtually all tactical folders are made with only one blade. All folders that I am aware of that qualify as survival folders are single bladed—with the exception of certain SAKs (Swiss Army Knives). I regard most SAKs as pocket-sized tool kits rather than folding survival knives. But a slip joint SAK will serve as well or better than my old Boy Scout knife. Much better are the models made by both Victorinox and Wegner, with locking main blades. These do qualify as survival folders. The blades are made of excellent stainless steel, the saws and other tools work well, and they are well made. If I had to, I could get along with one of the SAKs with one-hand-opening-and-locking main blade, a flint stick, and a watch-pocket-sized sharpening stone.

▲ Top: Victorinox Swiss Army Forester, Bottom: Victorinox Swiss Army Soldier's Knife.

The Two Knife Solution

While the medium to large knife is the most versatile and perhaps best single choice for an all-around survival knife, few can conveniently carry such a knife on their person except while in the bush. Also, the smaller knife is quite handy for the small tasks that make up a good bit of the work usually done with a survival knife, while the big knife will do big jobs faster and easier than a small or medium knife. As a result, many professionals, including survival instructors, daily carry a small fixed blade or a survival-quality folder on their person and a larger knife in their ready bag. It's a sound strategy that might work for you also.

The Finnish Leku, a knife that has a blade between seven and nine inches, is often sheathed with a smaller knife with about a three-inch blade. The Nepalese kukri, a large heavy knife with a blade in the nine- to twelve-inch range, is also often set up with a second smaller knife in the same sheath. This approach, two knives in one sheath, can be practical arrangement for bush knives.

Improvised Knives

Lacking any kind of knife, a survivor can craft an improvised cutting tool from stone, bone, glass, a tin can, or other scrap metal—depending on available materials. An explanation of flintknapping, the art of making stone tools, is beyond the limits of this book. But a sharp edge can often be made on a rock by chipping and scraping. In wilderness and fringe areas, bones can often be found if you're observant. They too can be made into functional tools. Tin cans and discarded bottles are, unfortunately, to be found in many wilderness areas and in fringe areas around the world. A half hour's work with any of these materials can produce a working blade. Examples are shown in accompanying photographs.

I crafted the bone knife shown from a whitened and well-chewed lamb shank bone I found in a Bulgarian forest while woods wandering. Most likely the lamb had been taken by a pack of European jackals. Bulgaria has the largest population of jackals in Europe, and I often heard them howling at night in that area. After splitting the shank between two large stones, I ground it to shape on first a rough stone and

▲ Bone knife made by author.

then a smoother one. Wrapping willow bark around the haft made a workable handle. This knife won't win any admiration from primitive skills experts and will not equal a steel knife in performance, but it is sharp enough to cut meat, hide, and wood. And I made it in about thirty minutes.

I cannot grace the sharp-edged rock in the photo with the term "knife." It would be a crude embarrassment to a master flintknapper, which I am not. But it will cut and I made it by chipping and scraping in only a few minutes.

Anyone who's ever cut a finger on a tin can lid can testify to its sharpness. A tin can lid bent to provide a handle makes a homely but functional cutting implement. Everyone's seen the movie scene where the bad guy breaks a bottle and attacks the good guy with its sharp broken edge. It's not only bad guys in movies who can use the edge of a broken bottle, however. To safely break a bottle to produce a usable blade, first score it with a rock in the shape you want. Then wrap it in something protective, such as clumps of weeds or leaves. Tap it lightly along

©ML Ayres

▲ Example of rock with sharp edge.

the scored lines. Done carefully, you shouldn't cut yourself and it should break, leaving you a super sharp but fragile cutting edge. Obsidian, which Native Americans used for knives and arrowheads, is nothing more than volcanic glass. Skilled flintknappers can and do make graceful and beautiful blades and arrowheads from common glass as well as obsidian.

None of these improvised blades will equal a steel blade in toughness or general service, but they are much better than nothing. Except for the tin can lid, our distant ancestors got along with similar blades for thousands of years.

Cost, Quality, and What Works for You

Considering that your life may depend on it, it's best to buy the highest quality survival knife you can obtain. Quality and cost do not always go together, but they often do.

Back in the sixties, when I first arrived at Smoke Bomb Hill, home of Special Forces (Green Berets), a senior sergeant advised me to buy a Randall, an expensive semi-custom knife, one of the few available then. Inexpensive commercial knives of that era simply were not up to the demands of Special Forces. Due to the nature of their missions, there is no military unit that

▲ Obsidian blade knapped by Jim Riggs with elk-antler handle, cutting beef.

places more importance on the survival knife, or makes more demands of a knife, than Special Forces. I had some idea of what lay ahead of me and I took the sergeant's advice. The Randall, a Model One, cost me almost a month's jump pay, not a small amount for a young soldier. I never regretted that purchase. That Randall served me reliably for daily tasks and field use for many years, and on more than one occasion proved its worth in life-threatening circumstances.

A Randall Model One might not be a good choice for you. Like the young NGO worker whose organization didn't allow him a fixed blade, your best choice for an everyday carry survival knife might be a Swiss Army Knife. Or, if you were in a similar position to the NGO worker, you might choose to ignore those regulations and carry a small fixed blade discreetly.

You should make your choices based on sound information, such as in this book, and according to your specific needs.

Today there are hundreds of top-quality choices available from limited-production specialty cutlers, and from some custom makers, at prices that are reasonable, given the quality of materials, often including exotic steels, and the amount of hand work that goes into them. However, those knives might be beyond the financial means of many. Fortunately, there are now available many perfectly functional and reliable knives made in large quantities of well proven and inexpensive materials by well-established factories. Detailed information on specific models is in another section of this book.

In selecting your survival knife or knives, keep in mind that that there are no magical

▲ Author's modified Randal Model 1 with hat.

knives that will, say, cut through a steel door and still be sharp enough to shave with. All knives are a compromise between various features: sharpness, cutting ability, edge holding, overall strength, ductility, weight, balance, and so on. A blade optimized for cutting ability and edge holding will of necessity be quite hard at the edge, which makes the edge subject to chipping under hard use or if it strikes, say, a stone. A blade that is not so hard at the edge will likely bend other than chip if it strikes a stone, but will not hold an edge as well. A blade that is too soft will not take a good edge. When selecting your knife, consider the maker's stated purpose for the knife and its design parameters. A katana (samurai sword), although it might be sharp as a three-foot long razor, is not a good tool for cutting through a steel door. A four-inch bladed utility knife is not the best choice for hacking tropical vegetation. It's best to consider your needs, pick a high-quality maker, trust what they say about their knives, then test them yourself.

Although it would be ideal to have a purpose-designed survival knife with you at all times, it might not be possible. The first and most important knife you select should be one that fits into your daily life. As in some of the incidents recounted at the beginning of this book, and in some later in this book, many people have saved themselves from injury or death with ordinary knives, "the knife they had with them."

Chapter Three

Sheaths and Carry Methods

Sheaths, which carry fixed-blade knives and some folders, are made from various materials. There are four things that are important for a sheath:

- It must hold the knife securely so that it doesn't fall out.
- It must be designed so that the blade doesn't cut through the material.
- It must hold the knife securely to the body when worn.

- It should be comfortable to wear.
- In addition, and this is critically important, a sheath should allow the knife to be withdrawn and replaced without the user having to look at the sheath. Looking at a sheath rather than your surroundings can break situational awareness, which could be critical. Few sheaths are designed to allow this.

▲ Kydex sheaths come in all sizes and shapes.

Strong, safe, comfortable sheaths are made from Kydex, a stiff plastic-like material, and similar synthetics, and from leather. Both have pros and cons.

Kydex is a sheath material popular with makers and users of military and survival knives. Properly made, it will stand up to hard use, secure the knife, and protect the user. Kydex is desirable if you expect to be in a humid or wet environment. It doesn't retain water like leather and therefore doesn't promote corrosion.

A well-made leather sheath is handsome, strong, and secure. It is also quiet, and makes no noise when worn or when a knife is withdrawn from it or resheathed. Kydex, being stiff and hard, will make noise if bumped with something hard, and often when a knife is withdrawn from it.

Leather sheaths sometimes have a hard synthetic liner to prevent the point from punching through. Most have a welt that runs around the edge of the sheath and which prevents the knife edge from cutting through the sheath and the point punching through.

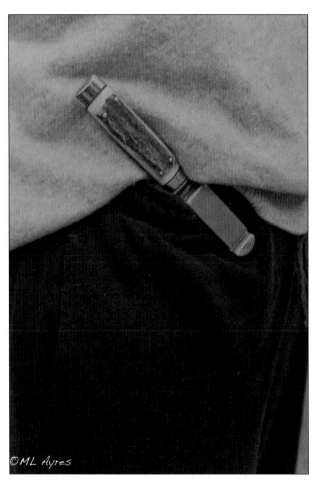

▲ Puma boot knife, sheath carried inside waistband.

▲ Wayne Goddard's Camp Knife; leather sheath with keeper carried inside back waistband.

Kydex sheaths usually prevent their knives from falling out by having a tight, molded fit. Leather sheaths accomplish this by using a retraining strap, or in the case of a pouch sheath, by having the knife seated deeply in the sheath and the sheath molded to the knife.

Survival knife sheaths are most commonly worn on the belt, where the knife can be easily reached. Some prefer strong side carry, others prefer cross carry. Belt attachments include loops and clips, which hold the knife and sheath close to the body. "Danglers" are sheaths that attach to the belt loosely and swing freely. This type of sheath can be comfortable to wear in the outdoors but may get hung up on shrubbery, or when entering or exiting vehicles.

Neck Knives

Carrying a utility knife with a four- to five-inch blade in a sheath worn on a strong cord (usually 550 parachute cord) around the neck is currently popular with some survivalists. Such knives carried in this way are called "neck knives," an imprecise term at best. You could tie a rope to a bayonet or a butter knife and hang it around your neck and call it a neck knife. In any event, carrying a sizable utility/survival knife in this way is neither safe nor secure.

I've been experimenting with knives carried around the neck since a certain bushcraft instructor began promoting the notion to the survival community back in the eighties. Within limits, this is an acceptable carry method; the limits being that the person is sedentary and that the knife is carried on a dog tag chain, which will break at twenty-seven pounds of pressure, rather than paracord at 550 pounds of breaking strength.

If the person carrying such a knife around his neck is at all active, runs, jumps, or might need to do so, neck-knife carry can lead to serious injury. I would no more wear paracord around my neck than I would a garrote or a noose, which is what that cord amounts to if it hangs up on any protrusion while you're moving fast, or if an enemy were to grab it in a tussle.

You might not live in an environment where you need to concern yourself with the possibility of an assailant approaching you from behind, or turning after walking past you, grabbing that cord around your neck, twisting it, and using it for a shoulder throw and/or to choke you into unconsciousness, or to death. Many people do.

More prosaically, the cord can catch on a tree branch or a part of a vehicle, tightening the cord about the neck and causing injury to the wearer. If the wearer is running, jumping, or doing much of anything other than sitting around a campfire, the knife and sheath will flop around uncontrollably, causing distraction, possibly leading to a fall, and increasing the odds that it will catch on something resulting in what rock climbers call a "static belay"—a hanging.

Several years ago, one of my correspondents was wearing one of these knives in this manner while exiting a pickup truck. The cord caught on the edge of the door, jerking him up and straining his neck. At the same time the knife went flying from its sheath and sliced across a friend's throat who was standing near the door. Fortunately, it was a shallow cut that was taken care of with first aid. My correspondent's neck required some first aid to take care of the area where skin had been torn away, and a half-dozen visits to a chiropractor to get the kinks out of his neck. He told me he would *never* again carry any knife in that manner.

Much more serious, and potentially calamitous, another correspondent when exiting an up-armored Humvee under enemy fire damn near broke his neck when his neck knife, which was suspended on paracord, hung up on a protrusion. During the time it took him to free himself, he was prevented from seeking cover from enemy fire. This was a massive failure of method that could have led to his death. Fortunately, he wasn't hit, but that was a matter of luck. His neck was severely injured and he was medevacked from the area to a field hospital. He had to wear a neck brace for weeks, and still, some years later, suffers from neck pain.

Another danger is that, in a fall, the knife/sheath combination can impact the ground or other surface while perpendicular to the wearer, resulting severe injury. I've seen this happen. In addition, a correspondent wrote me that he tripped and fell while running, the knife and sheath swung out from his chest—even though under his shirt—and when he hit the ground it struck him vertically in the breast bone, resulting in an injury requiring hospital treatment, even though the blade did not penetrate the sheath.

I've read other reports such as these from active-duty military people, and others, and have done a good bit of experimentation. There are additional reasons why I do not and will not carry such a knife around my neck, even if on a chain:

- If worn outside the shirt, it is visible to all, which is unacceptable in most places.
- If worn inside the shirt, it requires two hands to access the blade, and two hands and eyes

on to re-sheath, which is unacceptable to me in all instances.

- When so carried, the knife and sheath move about, rather than being in a fixed location where I can put my hand on it without fumbling or looking at it, which is also unacceptable.

There is one exception to my objections to so-called neck knives. A very small knife, such as Fred Perrin's Shark or Spyderco's ARK, if worn in a Kydex sheath, if worn under clothing, and if carried on a ball chain like a "dog tag" chain, can be a useful second or third or hideout blade. Such small knives are about the size of actual dog tags and are not subject to the same dangers as larger knives in that they move about under the clothing like dog tags and are unlikely to cause injury to the wearer. If the chain hangs up on something, it will break before causing injury. Importantly, wearing such a small second, third, or hideout knife in this manner can insure that it is always with you, like dog tags, which are meant to identify the wearer in extremis. Having such a knife at all times might prove to be critical insurance. I've used one of Fred Perrin's Sharks with a tiny flint stick as an igniter to make fire, to make a fuzz stick for that fire, and to sharpen spears and arrows, split feathers for fletching, and to dress small game. The Spyderco ARK was designed with a special steel so that it could be worn even while showering. This in response to American soldiers, men and women, being attacked and raped in the shower by groups of locals in Afghanistan. The ARK is also a useful utility knife. One of my friends, a former British SAS (Special Air Service) soldier, wears an ARK daily and uses it for many work-a-day tasks while remodeling homes. Both of these knives, and others in this category, can be effective survival tools and weapons and I have no reservations about carrying them in this manner.

Hideout Knives

Minuscule knives, such as those mentioned in the section on Neck Knives, and Tiny Knives, can be lifesavers—if you work for an NGO in a high-threat zone, or travel in one, or are active-duty military, or engaged in any activity that makes you a candidate for kidnapping, or if you simply forgot to carry your everyday survival knife and became lost in wilderness or caught in a disaster zone.

These tiny fixed blades can be tucked away in a money belt, or sewn into a hat or other clothing or into a boot or shoe. The tiny folders can be clipped to undergarments, socks, inside a hat, or other inconspicuous places. If

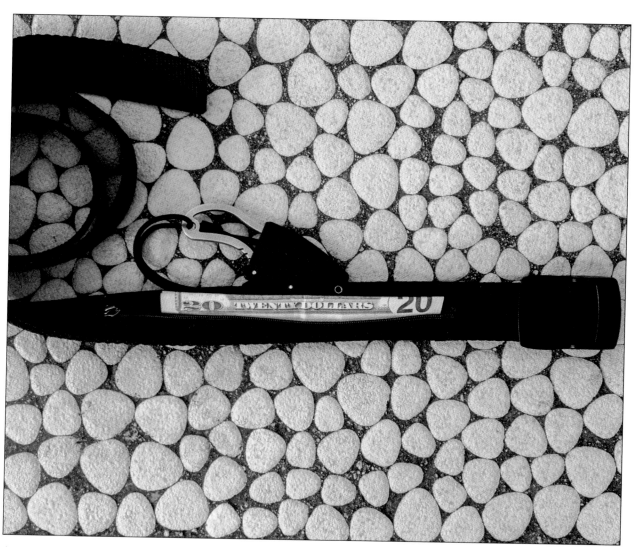

▲ CRKT RSK MK5 slipped inside a money belt.

the placement of the knife is comfortable and presents no obstacle to constant carry, you will likely have it with you at time of need. Either folder or fixed blade can prove to be a lifesaver.

Our far-distant ancestors survived and prospered with stone knives having blades of no more than an inch or so. With these small blades they dressed game, processed hides for clothing, fibers for shoes and baskets, and made shafts for arrows, javelins, and spears, and hafts for larger tools and weapons such as axes. I've done the same. So can you.

For comments on self-defense with a small blade, see the chapter on that topic. Also, I refer you to the section on self-defense in *The Tactical Knife*, which illustrates a method I've taught in many classes utilizing only knives with blades less than two inches in length. In some ways these small knives are, with a minimum of training, superior to large knives in the role of basic self-defense.

Chapter Four

Materials, Design, and Construction of the Survival Knife

urpose-designed survival knives should fulfill all the requirements previously discussed with ease. To do so, the following things must be considered by the maker:

- Selection of steel
- Heat treat appropriate to the steel being used
- Geometry of the blade
- Overall design of the knife

All these things must work together to produce a good survival knife, and how they come together determines the quality and performance of the knife. Many experienced knife users like to discuss steel selection and all of the technical details that go into the making of a good knife, just as auto enthusiasts like to discuss technical details of their favorite cars. However, just as few auto enthusiasts are capable of building a car from scratch or understanding all of the engineering that goes into automobiles, few knife users can make a knife or have a deep understanding of metallurgy or knifemaking. Nor do they need to. Here's some basic information on steel, blade geometry, and design to give you a grounding and to help you decide which knife, or knives, is right for you. If you're not interested in the technology you can skip this section.

Blades

Steel

There has been a continuing quest for better steel for blades since the late Bronze Age. As a result, today we have available some pretty good knife steels, including but not limited to: 1095, 01, A2, W2, D2, L6, 440B, 440C, ATS34, 5160, VG-10, 154CM, CPMS30V, and CPMS35V. These cutlery steels are alloys of basic elements and are supplied by steel mills and optimized for different features. For example, 1095, 01, and A2 are high-carbon tool steels, and with the proper heat treat, and in the right hands, become tough blades that take and hold sharp edges. Other steels, such as 440C and VG-10, have chromium added to their alloy, are rust resistant, and are tough and capable of taking and holding sharp edges. Still others, such as CPMS30V, are powder steels optimized for use as knives and considered by some to be super-steels. Not all agree.

Individual knifemakers have their own opinions as to which steel offers them optimal performance. Many knifemakers use a variety of steels, choosing each one for its best properties and the customer's intended use. The best steel for any knife is dependent on all the components that go into the knife, and the purpose for which the knife is designed. There is no definitive best steel.

Heat Treating

Rockwell hardness, which you will see quoted by knifemakers in their literature, is a measurement of the steel's hardness after it has been heat treated and finished. The higher the number, the harder the blade. In general, harder blades can take sharper edges and hold them longer, in some cases at the expense of being brittle and less tough. Balancing these properties is a function of heat treating. Again, it's a matter of trusting the knifemaker to get it right.

Grinds

Blades of survival knives, generally speaking, have one of the following profiles:

- **Flat grind:** The sides of the blades are tapered from spine to edge bevel. This produces a strong blade that cuts smoothly and well from spine to edge.

- **Saber grind:** This grind is flat from the spine to about halfway down the side of the blade, then tapered in a v grind to the bevel. Due to having thicker steel on part of the blade, the saber grind is strong and is often used for military knives. The thicker portion of the blade can drag in deep cuts in resistant material, such as wood. But good design offsets much of this effect.

- **Scandi grind:** This is basically the same as the saber grind, but with no secondary bevel. This design can produce somewhat less drag than the saber grind and, depending on exact angles, can be very

©ML Ayres

▲ Different grinds, left to right: Mora-Scandi grind, Spyderco Para-Military-flat grind, Chris Reeve Professional Soldier-hollow grind, Wayne Goddard Custom-convex grind.

controllable for shallow woodwork, such as making fuzz sticks. As a result, it is much favored by bushcrafters.

- **Convex grind:** The sides of the blade are ground from the spine to the edge in a smooth convex curve. Having a smooth curve from edge to spine, the convex grind cuts smoothly and does not bind or drag in deep cuts. It retains its edge very well and, due to its geometry, is the strongest edge. It is used on axes and on many hand-forged blades.

- **Hollow grind:** The sides of the blade are ground from the spine to the edge in a smooth concave curve. This grind removes steel from the sides of the blade and reduces drag for shallow cuts and scraping—thus its use for straight razors.

©ML Ayres

▲ Fred Perrin's Shark–Tanto, a chisel grind tiny blade.

It tends to bind in deep cuts and, due to having much steel removed, is not as strong as the other grinds.

- **Double edge:** With cuts on both edges of the blade, this was designed for weapon use and can lead to injuries in survival situations if the user is not completely familiar with it.
- **Chisel grind:** This is ground on only one side of the blade. It is commonly believed that this grind produces a stronger and sharper edge. This is a misconception. This edge, although used in many "tactical knives," tends to make the blade swerve to one side in deep cuts. Such a grind is optimal for slicing on one side of the material, as a chef does with a sushi knife.

Blade Points

Most survival knives have one of the following profiles:

- **Straight:** The sharp edge curves upward to meet the straight spine of the blade. Common on Scandi blades.
- **Clip:** The spine of the blade is "clipped" so that it meets the edge, usually at the blade's mid-point. This point is characteristic of Bowie knives, and is used for the KA-BAR and Pilot's Survival knives.
- **Drop point:** The spine curves down to meet the edge, often somewhat above the mid-point of the blade. Often used for hunting knives because the blade can cut edge-up when cutting into the chest or abdominal cavity of game animals.

▲ Bud Nealy Kwaiken with a tanto point blade. Photo credit: Bud Nealy.

- **Spear point:** Resembles the drop point but the top curve meets the edge at the mid-point of the blade. The spear point is used for Swiss Army Knives, and many others.
- **Tanto point:** A wedge-shaped point, all straight lines, no curves, was designed for armor-piercing centuries ago when metallurgy was not well developed, later superseded. It is used on a few knives which, if properly designed and made, can be functional.

Tangs

The tang is the portion of the knife that extends into the handle. A full-slab tang is considered the strongest because the least amount of steel is removed to make it. Some full-slab tangs are tapered and/or have holes drilled in them to improve balance. This is desirable, especially in a short-bladed knife, as they will tend to be handle heavy if they have an un-tapered full-slab tang.

A "rat tail" or stick tang is tapered very narrow to a shape suggested by its name. Many

▲ Blade points: Fållkniven Professional Hunter with an upswept point, Bark River Aurora with a spear point blade, Mora with a clip point blade, and Condor Bushcraft with a straight point blade.

▲ Fållkniven S1 full-tang knife.

◀ Pilot Survival Knife and KA-BAR both have full-stick tangs.

today consider the rat tail or stick tang to be weak. This is a misconception. Historically, most tangs of most edged tools and weapons have been of stick or rat tail design. The failure rate of such tangs is very low, even in hard use such as sword-to-sword impact. Both the KA-BAR and the Pilot's Survival Knife have full rat tail tangs.

Stick or rat tail tangs can extend the full length of the handle, or not. Partial tangs are common and, in a well-made knife, are quite functional. Many much favored bushcraft knives, such as the "Mora," have partial stick tangs.

Taper

A distal taper is one where the blade tapers from the hilt to the point. If properly done, the distal taper produces a well-balanced blade. It is often used in Bowies.

A profile taper narrows abruptly from a full thickness flat blade to the point. It is often used with a Scandi grind.

Handles and Guards

Handles come in all sizes and shapes and are made from materials ranging from wood, to antler, to synthetics. There are three things that are critical for handle shape:

- Security: A survival knife handle must be secure so that your hand will not slip, possibly onto the blade, and cause injury. Some handles are made of soft grippy synthetics, such as the Fällknivens; others have sculpted finger recesses, such as Fred Perrin designs; still others, such as the KA-BAR, use ridges along with rough leather to keep the hand from slipping. Guards are also, on some knives, used as a safety measure to prevent the hand from sliding onto the blade. Double guards, originally designed to aid in parrying an opponent's blade in combat, get in the way of close work and have no function on a survival knife. Single guards, if not too large, are desirable. The barrel-shaped handles seen on some Mora knives without a guard are not secure. These knives were originally designed as kitchen and general utility knives, and have recently become popular with bushcraft enthusiasts. Many expert primitive survival instructors have adapted them, due to low cost, their good steel, and the fact that they have been highly promoted by a well-known bushcraft instructor. These knives are excellent for

▲ Spyderco Fred Perrin Street Beat with sculpted finger recess.

small woodworking but are not suitable for all-around survival use, especially in the hands of a person with limited experience.

- **Durability:** Handles should not break or fall apart.
- **Comfort:** Handles should be comfortable for long sessions of hard work.

All of these features must be brought together to work in balance with each other, which requires much skill. Highly skilled knifemakers spend years learning their trade. In the right hands a lump of raw steel and a few other bits and pieces can become a world-class blade. The best survival knives come from the best makers—not always the most expensive ones. Do your research, starting with this book, select those that appear to best meet your needs, then use them to see if your selections are what you really need.

Chapter Five

Basic Use of Your Survival Knife

Simple Rules for Knife Safety

Always direct your attention to the edge and point of your blade and to whatever you are cutting.

- Cut away from your body, not toward it.
- Do not cut toward another person.
- Do not leave a knife on a work surface where it can get knocked off.
- In the field, your knife should be in your hand or in its sheath.
- If you drop your knife, let it fall. Do not attempt to catch it.
- Sharp knives are safer than dull ones because dull edges tend to slip. However, a sharp knife can cut deeply. Know your edge and what it will do.
- Keep knife handles clean, and do not let them get slippery.

Edge and Point Awareness

Use of a survival knife, or indeed any knife, will be safer, more effective, and efficient if you direct your attention to the edge and point when you are using them. By focusing your attention on the edge when, say, carving the belly of a bow or shaving tinder, or while slicing a tomato or a piece of meat, you will come to *feel* the edge as it cuts into the material on which you're working. If you direct your attention to the point of your blade, you will *feel* it as it pierces material, whether meat, bone, a coconut, the skin of a deer, or a round of Brie. This edge and point awareness will make you

a safer knife handler, preserve the sharpness of your knife longer, and you will learn how to get the most out of your knife with the least effort.

To develop edge and point awareness, get your knife and the material to be cut and a place to work, then clear your mind of distractions before beginning the task. Then focus tightly on the edge and point of the knife as you work with it. Feel how the edge cuts into the material on which you're working. Some edges are "toothy" and cut almost like a microscopic saw. Others are smooth and so sharp they seem to glide through the material with no resistance. Still others might be too smooth and slide on the material, not cutting efficiently. Some points will pass into and through various materials as if there was no resistance. Others will require some force.

Of course, the material upon which you're working will make a difference. Domestic beef is easier to cut than wild game, which is easier to cut than pine, which is easier to cut than oak. Pay close attention as you work on different materials and become familiar with how your knife behaves with each one.

If you extend this awareness to your knife when it's not in use, you will also come to know where it is at all times: in its sheath, or on that tree stump where you set it down. This will make you less likely to lose your survival knife, the loss of which could be a disaster.

The primary reasons to develop edge and point awareness, and to use your survival knife in the kitchen and around home, is to familiarize yourself with its performance, and by tightly focusing your attention on the edge of the blade as it cuts the material, become more efficient in its use, skills that could be critical in the field.

Everyday Use of your Survival Knife

Many advocate packing your survival knife in a survival kit to be set aside and only used in an emergency. The argument in favor of this is that the knife, and other gear, will be in good condition and ready for use in an emergency. There is some merit in this, if you're well practiced in the actual use of your knife and the other gear, and if you have two identical survival knives, one to keep with your gear for emergencies and one to use regularly. It's one thing to store, say, water purification tablets, quite another to store your survival knife, your most important tool. Storing a knife you've never used, or only used casually for familiarization, might easily result in inefficient use, or in cutting yourself, which in a survival situation could endanger your life.

Imagine cutting through, say, a willow shaft, which is a soft wood, with a razor-sharp knife you've only used a couple of times. Perhaps you didn't realize how easy it would be to cut willow with your knife and you cut into it with force, applying so much force that you cut through the shaft and into your thigh where the shaft is braced. Say you cut deep into your thigh and sever your femoral artery. Now you've got a major artery spurting out your life's blood at an alarming rate. A moment ago you were working to solve a survival problem, making a hunting weapon by crafting a spear, bow, arrow, or throwing stick. Now you have a life-threatening emergency and only seconds to resolve it before you lose consciousness, bleed out, and die.

Less dramatically, if you're not familiar with your most basic and important tool, your survival knife, you might waste precious time learning how to split open wet wood to get to the dry center, how to shave wood curls and scrape wood dust for tinder, while the temperature is dropping, snow is falling, and night is coming on. Cutting meat will familiarize you with the processes required to dress game. Cutting vegetables in your kitchen will help prepare you to deal with foraged wild food. Woodwork of all kinds will build the skills to safely and efficiently craft primitive tools and weapons and build shelters.

Being unfamiliar with your survival knife will not serve you well in an actual survival situation and could lead to non-survival. You will be better served if you use your survival knife frequently, become intimately familiar with it, learn what it can and cannot do, and become highly proficient in its use. Begin by doing so in your own home and by focusing your attention on your work. By working with your knife, you will also discover its characteristics, and deficiencies, if any.

The Cuts

To use a survival knife effectively, you must be proficient in its use. This would appear to be obvious, but in today's mostly urban world many people have had no basic training in knife usage.

The Draw Cut: Place the edge of your blade on the material you want to cut and draw the edge across it while maintaining downward pressure. Often the draw cut is confused with sawing, which is ineffective with a blade lacking

▲ Using the CRKT Hissatsu on a roast chicken to illustrate a draw cut.

saw teeth. The draw cut differs from sawing in that, when sawing, you draw the saw teeth of your blade back and forth over the intended cutting surface with little downward pressure. Press down firmly and draw your blade toward you. The draw cut is the most effective cut for soft materials, and is the most common cut used by butchers and sushi chefs

The Push or Press Cut: This cut can be used to bring down a small sapling when you have only a small knife. In the instance of cutting through a sapling, bend the sapling and apply the edge of your blade to the outside of the bend. Press down with a good bit of pressure.

As the blade cuts into the wood, rock the edge back and forth slightly. On other materials, simply place your edge on the material and firmly press down until your blade parts the material.

The point can also be used with a press cut. Instead of striking with force, as with a stab, place the point on the object you wish to penetrate and press down. This is useful when, for example, you need to dig into a dead log to get to dry wood, or to start a hole you want to ream or drill, as when starting a socket in a friction fire board.

Drilling and/or Reaming: Press the point of your blade into the surface to be drilled, then

▲ Fållkniven PXL/Ivory Micarta illustrating a press cut.

turn the blade into the direction of the edge. After making some progress, reverse and turn the edge in the other direction. To continue, press down into the cavity and turn the blade, reversing the edge as needed.

The Shear Cut: Anchor the tip of your knife so it does not move, often with the heel of your off hand. Holding the handle in the other hand, use the secured tip as a fulcrum and press down with your edge on the material to be cut. The shear cut can also be combined with the draw cut in a kind of rocking motion. An example of this can be seen by watching any experienced chef.

The Slash: Usually done with speed, the slash is simply moving your edge to and through the material to be cut in a sweeping motion. Using a speedy slash to open a cut, then using a draw cut to cut deep is taught in certain blade arts and is a highly effective technique. If you have the opportunity to watch a kenjutsu practitioner, note that what begins as a slash is often converted to a draw cut when the edge of their sword penetrates the object they are cutting, usually rolled rice mats. Do not confuse kenjutsu with kendo. Kendo is practiced with shinai, which are made up of bamboo slats bound

▲ Spartan Enyo drilling holes for a fire board.

together with leather. Shinai have no edge. In general kendo "cuts" are actually strikes, which amount to a whack or a hit, not a cut. Kenjutsu is traditional Japanese swordsmanship.

The Stab: Secure the handle firmly in your hand—sometimes, depending on the configuration of the handle, by wrapping your thumb over the butt, or heel, of the handle—and forcefully drive the point of your blade into that which you wish to penetrate. You might use a stab to penetrate the wall of a room or auto in which you are trapped. After stabbing into plaster, or sheet metal, you can use a combination of other cuts, shear cuts, press cuts, batoning, and so on to enlarge the opening enough to escape.

The Chop: Swing your edge with force into the material to be cut. Keep your wrist loose and allow the blade to whip into the object you are cutting

Well-designed medium-sized blades, six to seven inches long, can be somewhat effective as choppers. No medium-sized knife can equal a big knife with a nine- to twelve-inch blade, a machete, or a hatchet, as a chopper, but chopping with a medium-sized blade can

▲ AG Russell fixed blade illustrating a slash cut through one-inch hanging hemp rope.

◀ Illustrating the stab.

shorten the time required to accomplish a task. The best edge for chopping is the convex edge, which offers little resistance to the material being cut after opening the cut. Also, the convex edge better supports the edge against the massive force applied during a chop. Chopping with, say, a hollow-ground edge, even with a large blade, can damage the edge

The convex edge is used on many well-designed knives and virtually all machetes, hatchets, and axes. You can increase the chopping effectiveness of a medium-sized knife, or a large one, by gripping the handle at about the halfway mark, with your little and ring fingers over the butt. This increases your leverage. It can be a good idea to use a lanyard while doing this, unless you're using a Leku with a ridge at the butt that can be grasped, thereby securing the knife in hand. Chopping with a small knife with a three- to five-inch blade, is futile, ineffective, and damaging to the edge of the knife. Instead of attempting to chop with a small knife, use a baton.

Batoning

If you need to chop things and have only a small knife, always use a baton. Batoning is a highly effective technique for cutting large things with a small knife. Since most of us are equipped with only a small knife most of the time, I consider batoning to be a critical survival skill. A baton is anything sturdy that can be used to pound a blade through a resistant medium: a chair or table leg, a large or small steel flashlight, even a hard-soled shoe will serve. In one of the incidents mentioned in the introduction, where the firefighter rescued the injured and trapped woman from a steel shipping container, he used a chunk of concrete as a baton. In another, a traveler used the sole of a hard shoe with his knife to cut a hole in a steel fire door and allow many people to escape a fire in a high-rise building. A baton can also be used with medium and large knives to increase power.

Correctly done, batoning will not damage the knife—if the knife is well constructed and if you use proper technique. The basic method is to simply place your edge onto the thing you wish to cut and lightly but firmly strike the spine of the blade directly over the cutting surface—I repeat, lightly. Do not hit your blade like you're going for a home run. Hitting your blade too hard can result in damage. Continue striking the back of the blade until you accomplish your task.

Expanding on the basics, hold the baton in a loose pivot grip so that it can rotate around the junction of your fingers where you grasp it. Hold the knife with a loose but firm grip, so that it can pivot around the axis of your thumb and second finger. The other fingers should be somewhat loose. The knife must be able to pivot in order to avoid stress in the event of a misplaced strike. If using a folder, the key is not to put direct stress on the lock. No folder should be driven through a resistant medium point first, whereas a fixed blade can be.

To start, strike the back of the blade directly over the place where the edge is in contact with the surface to be cut. By striking in this spot you transfer the force of the blow through the blade and into the object you are cutting with very little stress on the blade. As your knife blade goes deeper into the material you're cutting, you may need to transfer your strike point to the forward portion of the blade—again, do so with light taps. Do not pound unless there is an

▲ DPx HEST splitting an oak log by batoning.

immediate emergency. Correct baton technique will stress your knife far less than chopping with it. This is because when chopping, the edge must absorb the energy of the strike. Chopping with a folder or small knife is ineffective in any event. If you use proper technique, batoning wood should not damage your knife, either fixed blade or tactical folder.

To cut through a flat surface, such as door, place the belly of the blade, just behind the point, on the surface. Again, strike directly above the contact point—until the point goes through the door, at which time you'll need to transfer your point of impact to that portion of the blade you can reach. Since you are using a curved part of the edge, the cut will be a bit easier than when you use the straight part of the edge.

You can use a baton when there is no ax or machete available and you need to cut saplings for an emergency shelter, or cut through a locked door to escape a burning building, or peel open a car body to extract a trapped passenger.

In the instance of the firefighter cited in the introduction, the firefighter was alone. He had

▲ Bushcraft shelter knife illustrating scraping.

none of the tools of his trade with him. He used his folder and a chunk of concrete to make two diagonal intersecting cuts, pulled the steel sheet out of the way, and rescued the woman. His folder was a "tactical folder" from one of America's leading manufacturers. Cutting steel like the firefighter did, especially using a chunk of concrete as a baton, may destroy your knife. But a knife is a small price to pay for a life.

Scraping: Scraping is moving the edge of your blade over the surface of an object with the edge held perpendicular to the work. Scraping is an important skill. You need to scrape the belly of a bow to refine it and the shaft of a spear to remove snags and smooth it. The back of a blade's point can also be used to scrape away mortar between bricks or concrete blocks to escape a collapsed building.

If you want to be prepared for a survival situation, practice batoning and all of these basic skills before you actually need to use them. Use your survival knife in the kitchen, to open boxes, cut cord, trim shrubbery, and other household tasks. Such daily use will build important familiarity. Don't wait until a building is burning down around you before you try to use a baton, or scrape mortar from between bricks, or break through a plaster wall, or cut through a steel metal door. Reading about how to do something is not the same as actually doing it. Be inventive. Use expedient batons. See how effective a steel flashlight is as a baton compared to, say, the hard heel of a shoe. Obviously, a sneaker would be less effective as a baton than a table leg. But in a recent test a small woman was able to cut through the roof of a car with a tactical folder and one of her boat shoes.

Try cutting different things, including tree limbs, discarded doors, plywood, and junked car bodies. You will learn about the resistance of various materials and become proficient in the skill. If you go at it seriously you may make a few mistakes; you may wreck a knife or two in the process. But that's a small price to pay to acquire valuable survival skills. Don't complain to the knifemaker if you destroy a knife while learning. Consider it the price of an education.

How to Sharpen and Maintain Your Survival Knife

Knives get dull from use because the edges wear down from abrasion with the materials being cut. To sharpen your blade, you must remove steel from the edges. To do this you will need a sharpening stone, which could be a natural stone, carborundum, or diamond. Blades can also be sharpened with emery paper and field expedients such as rocks. For hi-tech steels such SV30 you'll want a diamond hone to cut the steel more easily. Natural stone is fine for carbon steel blades. Some people use oil on their stones. I do not. I use water for all stones, diamond or natural, to float away steel particles that can clog the stone and render it inefficient.

There are sharpening devices available, such as Spyderco's TriAngle and EZE-LAP's guides, that make sharpening easy for the beginner, indeed for anyone. However, these devices are too bulky to carry afield. The survivor should practice with a pocket-sized stone until he can get a sharp edge with it. The most important thing is to keep a constant angle as you hone your blade. Visualize a small coin at the spine of your blade to help keep the edge at a constant angle.

If your blade has a convex grind, stroke the blade along the stone *away* from the edge. For any other kind of grind, stroke the edge *toward* the stone, as if cutting a thin slice. Keeping the stone wet as you work will aid in sharpening. Direct your attention closely to the edge as you work and you will soon see how the steel moves and how the edge is formed. If you have a leather belt, stropping a few strokes *away* from the edge will aid in putting a finished edge on any grind.

Carbon steel knives will discolor with use. This is not harmful to the blade. Rust is harmful. Avoid rust by drying your carbon steel blade after use. For the most part, hi-tech steels do not rust. They should, however, be cared for. Keeping your blade dry and clean after use is easy, and sound survival behavior.

Chapter Six

Field Use of the Survival Knife

Survival is often a matter of doing something critical and effective with the least amount of time and effort. Every task you undertake will consume time and energy, which must be replaced by food. For example, getting a fire going when you are soaking wet and cold is something that must be done quickly—and right. Trying to shortcut the process will usually result in failure. Successful fire making requires that each component be present, and that each essential step be followed. A good knife and practice will enable you to build a fire from available materials in the least amount of time possible.

However, as an old saying has it, "perfection can be the enemy of good enough." I have seen survival students, perhaps inspired by their instructor's well-crafted example, work for many hours, sometimes all day, to construct a shelter that they are going to occupy for only one night. Likewise, many will invest hours in making a simple spear: selecting just the right shaft to work with, smoothing and straightening the shaft and carving and sharpening the point until they have a museum-quality example of a primitive weapon. In a survival situation, this is a misallocation of precious resources: time and energy.

There are experts in primitive crafts who can turn out a finely crafted bow fit for museum display in a few hours. For the rest of us in a survival situation, however, good enough is good enough. Building a wilderness shelter in which you plan to spend only one night before moving on should occupy no more than an hour of your time. A serviceable spear can be crafted in ten to fifteen minutes. There is a narrow line between good enough and perfection that only experience can reveal. So, practicing survival skills with your knife when not under stress is survival behavior. When making a shelter or crafting hunting tools and weapons, remember that they are only a means to an end—survival—and that you have other tasks to accomplish, such as finding water, actually hunting with the tools you've made, securing game, and eventually returning to an environment that doesn't require living on the edge.

The right mental state to have is one of full awareness, curiosity, and confidence that you're at home on our planet and that, with effort and determination, you will prevail. Man versus wild attitudes are counterproductive and inappropriate. Nature is not against you. You are not in a fight with the natural world. Nor is the Bambi-like child of nature attitude useful. Nature is not your mother and will not take care of you. The natural world is neutral, a backdrop against which you play out the drama of your life. Keep your wits about you, blend and flow with your environment, and you can survive. Succumb to fear and you might not.

Making Fire

Fire can save your life. Fire can take your life.

Fire can warm you when you're freezing, disperse bugs when they're driving you buggy, signal for help, protect you from wild animals, make food safe to eat, cheer you when you're depressed, and reassure you when fearful. The ability to make fire is one of the things that defines us as humans. The ancients believed fire was a gift from the gods. They may have been right.

In wilderness survival, fire making is IT, your most critical skill. Before knowing how to build a shelter, before knowing how to make primitive tools, know how to make fire quickly and safely. Safety is simple: Clear the area where you will have your fire of combustible materials so that it will not get out of control and spread. Do not grab burning objects or put your hands in the fire. Do not fall or roll into your fire. That's mostly it for fire safety.

Building a fire is a little more complicated, but not so much so that a six-year-old who pays attention cannot master the art. Fire making seems to be a great mystery to many. It need not be. To build a fire, you only need:

- Igniter
- Tinder
- Kindling
- Fuel
- Oxygen
- Knowledge of how to use these things
- A knife helps too—considerably

An **igniter** can be a match, a lighter, a fire-steel or sparker, flint and steel, a flare, an electric

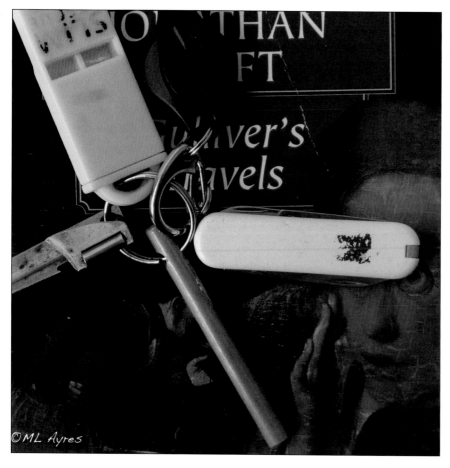

◀ Traveler's essentials: whistle, Photon Micro pinch light, Victorinox Classic with small, razor-sharp edge, fire steel, and P38 GI can opener.

▲ Igniter sources: a waterproof matchcase and a common cigarette lighter.

spark, a magnifying glass if there's sunlight, or a hot coal from another fire. You can also use friction—if you know how to generate enough heat by friction to get a coal, an advanced skill I will only touch on in this book.

Everyone who gives any thought to survival should always have at least two igniters on their person. Igniters are tiny, weigh next to nothing, could save your life, and are impossible to replace in the wilderness. They're also convenient for lighting your barbecue.

Fire-steels, or sparkers, are excellent igniters and throw a hot spark that will catch any good tinder. They are not rendered useless by water, as are matches, and are not affected by cold, as are butane lighters. Even the smallest fire-steel, one that can fit on your key ring, will last for thousands of uses. Simply scrape the back of your knife blade, or use the scratcher that comes with some fire-steels, the length of the fire-steel, throwing sparks into the tinder.

Butane lighters provide a flame rather than a spark. They will easily ignite tinder, and will ignite less-than-optimal tinder easier than a fire-steel. Like a fire-steel, they last for thousands of uses. The best quality lighters are reliable, although subject to be being affected by cold, as they will not ignite if they get too cold.

You can avoid this by carrying them inside your clothing when it's extremely cold.

Lighters that use fluid, such as the classic Zippo, have advantages over butane lighters in that they will ignite without respect to cold weather, and they will continue to burn without the necessity of holding down an ignition lever. Their disadvantage is that the fluid they use evaporates and must be refilled from time to time whether used or not.

Although they produce a flame, matches are the third or fourth choice as igniters. Their flame lasts only for a short time and even "waterproof" matches can fail if immersed in water. However, they are effective igniters and available almost anywhere.

Tinder is anything that that will easily catch fire and burn long enough and hot enough to start kindling burning. Paper, cloth, weeds, dry leaves, wood shavings, pine resin, Spanish Moss, tree fungus, bark, rotten wood, wood dust, fibers from a carpet, lint from a dryer—all can be used as tinder. Good tinder catches fire easily and must be dry. If you have nothing else, and if your clothing is dry, a strip of cotton or wool cloth from a shirt or sweater will serve.

©ML Ayres

▲ Sources of tinder: gathered pine cones, an aviator survival kit, and Esbit fuel tabs.

▲ Dried river cane leaves make great tinder.

Synthetic fabrics melt rather than burn and will not serve as tinder.

Kindling consists of small pieces of wood or other flammable material, anything that burns hot and long enough to start fuel burning. Wood kindling should be in graduated sizes, from toothpick to pencil to finger and up to wrist-sized. Other kindling, such as auto seat covers and seat belts, small rubber tubes, hose strapping and belts, carpet and upholstery strips, should be cut into graduated sizes before use. Kindling also needs to be dry.

Fuel is anything that will burn, with the most common fuel being wood. If wood is being used as fuel it should, like kindling, be gathered by size, or cut or split into graduated sizes, starting with wrist sized and going to larger if you want or need a large fire. Many of the things you can use as kindling, carpets and so on, can also be used for fuel in larger sizes. It's best if fuel is dry, but if you have enough kindling you can sometimes use damp fuel.

Oxygen is present all around us, but its lack is a common cause of failure in fire making. Piling too much kindling and fuel on tinder will smother the spark and initial flame.

Having a **knife** enables you to make tinder from wood scrapings, to shave "fuzz sticks" and curls from wood, to split kindling and small sticks of fuel from large chunks of wood, rip

▲ Gathered kindling ready to be added to a fire.

▲ Wayne Goddard's Camp Knife with split kindling.

open dead logs to get dry wood, and to cut carpets, auto upholstery, and inflammable trash such as boxes. If you don't have a knife, you'll need to find a sharp rock or make an edge on a rock.

Fire making is not difficult if you direct your attention to the details. Each component, in some form or another, *must* be present and each step *must* be followed to successfully build a fire. Many who have trouble starting a fire ignore or do not know these basics. Others know the basics in theory, perhaps from reading about them, but have no practical experience starting fires. The process is not especially difficult, and can be mastered to the degree that you can quickly start a fire under almost any conditions. But, as with many things, the devil is in the details.

I once met a cowboy—well, sort of a cowboy—one autumn deep in a wilderness area over twenty miles from the nearest road. The leaves had fallen, first frost had come and gone, and the temperatures were below freezing at night. My brother-in-law, George, and I were traveling on foot, exploring the area and doing a little fishing and small-game hunting along the way. We were sitting by our campfire one evening when we saw at some distance a man on horseback riding along the stream bed near which we had camped. He was headed in our direction.

We stood as he rode up to our camp and dismounted. He wore a big Stetson hat, a Levi jacket, jeans, cowboy boots, leather chaps, and a single-action .45 caliber revolver in a cowboy-style holster. He looked cold and hungry and his horse was tired. He asked if he could share our fire and get warm. Of course! We invited him to have a seat close to the fire and tossed some more wood on.

As we talked, I learned that he lived in a large city and stabled his horse in a small town near the wilderness area. He had always wanted to be a real cowboy and this was his first extended trip on his horse and his first trip into a wilderness area. He was "kinda turned around," and couldn't find the way back to the road and hadn't had a fire in days. He had camped in this same spot previously and had returned here because he was "near to freezing," and this was the last place he had been able to build a fire. For some reason he seemed to associate successful fire making with location rather than procedure. He was very interested in the topic of fire making and asked, "So you guys can just make a fire whenever you want?"

"Uh, yeah," George said. This led to a short demonstration. Cowboy—he told us to just call him "Cowboy" when I asked his name—had some trouble with the basic concepts and kept trying to ignite a fire by holding a kitchen match to a stick the size of his wrist. The only cutting tool he had was a little Barlow pocketknife with a two-inch blade that he carried in the watch pocket of his jeans, "like cowboys do." I went over the basic procedures a couple more times, and with my sheath knife again demonstrated how to split wood, make fuzz sticks, and make tinder from bark scrapings. After watching, he vowed to buy a "real knife" when he got back to town. I loaned him a spare knife to make tinder and kindling. Finally, as last light was fading, he managed to ignite a fire. We passed around a bottle of snake-bite medicine in celebration of Cowboy's newfound skill. Off to the side, George said to me, "I think this guy's seen too many movies." We invited him to join us for dinner.

Cowboy took a can of SPAM and some crumbled crackers from his saddlebag, and said it was all he had left. We told him to save it for his ride out and shared our dinner with him: two tough but tasty rabbits, corn cakes baked on a hot rock, and a salad of clover and watercress from the stream bank. We had been careful to clean any snail eggs, which uncooked can become internal parasites, from the watercress.

After dinner, some conversation, and a couple more doses of snake-bite medicine, Cowboy rolled up in his single wool blanket next to the fire. I was awakened about one o'clock in the morning for the fifth or sixth time by Cowboy rolling, tossing, and muttering. The temperature had dropped and it had started to snow. Soft fluffy flakes piled up on my tarp. Well, I thought, jeans and a single blanket and it's below freezing, and now snowing, anyone but an Eskimo would be cold. Cowboy had thrown logs on the fire until it looked like a stage one forest fire, but he was getting cooked on one side and frozen on the other, and that cold ground was just sucking the heat out of him. George sat up and said, "I can't take this anymore."

We got up, found a couple of long sticks and told Cowboy to get up and move away from the fire. He looked at us wide eyed, as if he thought we were going to beat him with the sticks. By now, what with our moccasins and other gear, and the ability to make fire, forage a little greenery and shoot rabbits with a bow, we had most likely in his mind taken on the aspect of wild men. Along with cowboy movies, maybe he had also seen *Deliverance*.

"Relax," George said. "We're gonna warm you up."

We poked the fire with our sticks and dragged burning wood and coals apart, making two fires about six or seven feet apart, each about five feet long. After making sure there were no coals left between the two fires, we raked an inch or so of dirt over that ground. "Now move your blanket and lay down on that warm ground between the two fires," I told Cowboy.

He had been watching us closely and keeping an eye on his .45, which was next to his saddle. But he was pale and shivering and I guess he decided we weren't going to burn him alive. He put his blanket down and laid where we told him and was soon warm enough to stop shivering. We told him to put small amounts of wood on the two fires as they burned down and he'd be good for the night. And he was.

The light snow didn't stick and morning brought bright, clear sunshine. We fed the happy cowboy hot oatmeal with walnuts and dried blackberries and sent him on his way with a map I drew on a page from my notebook.

Here's the point of that story: Learn how to build a fire. If you don't have any other wilderness skill, learn to make fire. It can save your life. Oh, and have a real knife.

To Build a Fire

Select a spot for your fire that is clear of debris, or clear a spot, so that your fire will not get out of control and spread. Before igniting a fire, gather all the materials and arrange them by size so you can add them as you progress. If the ground is wet, start your fire on a small platform of dry wood, or a dry rock if available.

Ignite the tinder and place it under the smallest kindling, which you have arranged as a tepee, log cabin, or other structure that allows air to flow freely around the kindling. When the smallest kindling catches, gradually

▲ Using a fire-steel and the back of a knife to strike sparks onto tinder.

◄ Sparks from fire-steel ignite the tinder.

Field Use of the Survival Knife •

add larger kindling until you have a good flame. Then, careful not to smother your fire, add fuel, starting with the smallest size and gradually increasing until you have the size fire you need.

Generally, for survival purposes, small fires are better than big ones. They consume less fuel, require less effort to maintain, and will keep you as warm as a large fire if you sit or stand close. Sometimes larger fires are needed, as in the case of the cowboy who couldn't build a fire and who didn't dress for the weather. Common sense and the immediate situation will guide you.

Fire making should go smoothly, even for the beginner, if conditions are optimal, if you have dry materials and a functioning igniter, if it hasn't been pouring rain and soaking everything in your environment, if you haven't fallen into an icy river and now you're wet and freezing and it's starting to snow. If conditions are not optimal, you'll have to try a little harder. If everything is soaking wet, and *if* you have a knife, you can rip open dead logs and split thick branches to get at dry material. If you don't have a knife, things are going to be much harder, doable probably, but harder.

Fire by Friction

If you lack a functional igniter, you'll need to make tools to create a fire by friction. Virtually all survival manuals explain and illustrate how to make fire by friction. What many of them do not tell you is that if you haven't practiced this skill and you find yourself in a survival situation, desperately needing fire, you're going to need patience, persistence, a good bit of energy, and some luck. Be prepared to sweat and to get blisters if your hands are keyboard soft.

Understand this: No friction fire method is as easy to use successfully as many survival books lead their readers to believe. Full instruction in all details is beyond the scope of this book. The easiest and most reliable friction fire methods I have used are these two: bow drill and the plough, and neither of them is easy. You'll need to use your knife to make these tools. Lacking a knife, you'll need to find a sharp rock, or chip a blade from stone, if any workable stone is available. Locating workable stone requires some knowledge, and you'll need some basic understanding of flint knapping best acquired from dedicated specialized books on primitive skills. Better yet, try to get some personal hands-on instruction from an experienced person. Easier to make is a bone knife as previously shown (page 30)—if you can locate some bone. Making fire from friction is difficult, especially for the novice. Add in making a field-expedient knife and you've got a steep hill of learning to climb.

For the bow drill, you need a fire board, drill, socket, bow, and cordage. Rather than making cordage for the drill, another time-consuming task, use a boot or shoelace, or that length of cord in your pocket.

For the plough, you need two pieces of wood (both dry), a flat surface with a groove, and a stick that fits into the groove. Rub the stick back and forth in the groove as if you're trying to make the groove deeper until friction creates wood dust and heat to make a coal.

All tools must be dry. If the ground is wet, you'll need to place some dry material between the fire board and the ground.

Despite my early interest in primitive outdoor skills, and despite many efforts, I was unable to successfully kindle fire by friction

▲ Using the point of the knife to drill holes for a fire board.

▲ Fire board and drill.

▲ Close-up of fire board and drill.

until receiving personal hands-on instruction from experienced people. This is not to discourage you, but to inform you that these skills are best learned in advance of need.

Your best plan is to have a knife and an igniter *at all times*, and to practice these other skills as a leisure activity. Do not wait until you've fallen in an icy stream miles from a road and with no knife or igniter to try making your first fire by friction.

If everything around you is wet, and you cannot locate dry materials for your friction fire tools, or if for whatever reason nothing works to start a fire, build a thick walled and floored shelter, crawl inside, and hope to dry out and get warm. But if you have a choice, don't bet your life on it. Fire is IT.

Hobo Stoves

Trash is so widespread that you can, and do, find discarded tin cans (also plastic bags and other trash) in all but the most pristine wilderness areas, including the middle of the Pacific Ocean, where gigantic rafts of trash float with

◄ Hobo camp stove lit with four knives in background: Condor Primitive Bush Knife, Fällkniven A1, Buck Compadre, and ESEE Junglas.

the currents. Developing countries are all but buried under mounds of plastic debris, bottles, and cans. It's a vexatious situation, but the survivor makes do and uses what's available.

A hobo stove is an improvised device made from a tin can. By concentrating the heat from a tiny amount of fuel, and by utilizing convection, a hobo stove can boil water to purify it, cook food, heat a shelter, and contain the fire safely. Hobo stoves can be made from any kind of can, and will burn almost anything combustible, including dried animal dung.

Making one is simplicity itself—if you have a knife. Usually, a scavenged can will have one end, the lid, removed. You can cut out the other end, leaving a metal tube open at both ends, or leave one end closed. Opening both ends gets more heat directly onto a cooking vessel, such as another scavenged can. A closed end provides a grill upon which you can cook directly. Either version will provide heat, but I prefer the latter version.

With either type, cut a door at the bottom of the can, the side that will be placed on the ground. Next cut a ventilation hole at the top of the can on the *opposite* side of the door. This ventilation hole will provide the updraft that will make the fire burn hot.

Kindle a small fire inside the stove, or on the ground first, then place the stove over the fire. Feed the fire with twigs, pine cones, bamboo scraps, or other fuel through the door. These simple devices work very well, much better than you might expect if you've never tried one. Similar and equally effective stoves can be made by mounding clay, or by piling rocks, in a similar structure. If rocks are used, clay or dirt must be packed into the chinks between rocks.

The key to creating a chimney effect, and making such stoves burn hot, is to provide ventilation at bottom and at the top.

Wilderness Shelter

The key point to keep in mind when building a survival shelter is that you need *shelter*, not a log cabin, a hunting camp, or a vacation home. Think nest: eagle, crow, or squirrel's nest; or den: fox, cougar, or bear's den. Think small. If alone, your shelter should be just large enough for you to fit inside, and with space for a tiny fire at the entrance. If not alone, your shelter should be just large enough for the number of people in your group. In temperate or cold environments, keeping warm is the primary purpose of a shelter. More is not needed. Other points:

- Use the materials close to hand.
- Invest no more time than necessary to build a nest.

If you're going to be spending longer than a night or two in one location, it might be worthwhile to add refinements to your shelter, as time allows. If moving on is your survival strategy, investing too much time in your shelter is not a good allocation of your resources.

The reasons for keeping your shelter small are:

- It requires less time and energy to build a small shelter.
- Small shelters can be heated with a tiny fire, which requires less time and energy to maintain.
- Small shelters will better hold your body heat.

A good rule of thumb is to invest no more than one hour in building a shelter, no matter how many people are to be provided for. One person spends one hour to build a tiny shelter for himself. Two people each spend one hour, and three still only spend one hour each. Thus, a one-person shelter will require one man hour, a two-person shelter two man hours, a three-person three man hours—but each would be built in one clock hour.

If you practice making shelters, and you should if you're interested in survival, you will quickly find which knife is the most efficient and enables you to construct a survival shelter in the least amount of time. In the accompanying photos, you will see shelters of various types being constructed. In some instances, large or medium fixed blades were used, tools that are much more efficient than small fixed blades or folders. In other instances, small blades or folders were used to demonstrate their usefulness. Over the years I have timed myself, and students, some of whom had no previous experience, while making shelters and primitive tools. In actual practice we have found that, all things being more or less equal, using a small knife, fixed blade or folder, will require about twice as much time to construct a shelter as using a medium-sized knife will, and about four times as much as using a large knife will, a difference that could be critical and should be allowed for. While the larger knife is more efficient and desirable, you may have only a small fixed blade or a folder. In such a case, you should make allowances for the limitations of your tools.

Site Selection

Proper site selection will save you time and energy, and save the edge of your knife. Find a site that provides adequate materials to build your shelter. The more materials available to be gathered without cutting or chopping, the better. Starting with a sheltering tree in the forest, a large boulder in the desert, or a grove of bamboo wherever it grows can save much work if you use those natural features as part of your shelter.

Generally speaking, I prefer to make survival shelters blend in with their surroundings. I prefer to be unseen unless I decide to be seen. That's partially military experience talking and partially experience of traveling in unfriendly areas. You may prefer to build your shelter so that it can be easily seen by rescuers. Almost any hidden shelter can be transformed into one that's easily found with the addition of green vegetation or other material to create smoke that can be seen from afar. Needs vary according to personal situations. Both types of shelters are shown in accompanying photos.

Shelter needs also vary a great deal according to area, climate, weather, and available materials. In cold climates you'll want to make the walls and floor as thick as possible, given time and material availability. In the desert you need shade from the sun in daytime. In swampy areas you'll want to build a platform to get off the ground.

The accompanying photos show a few shelters made for various climates. They were made with only a knife and the contents of my pockets or those of my students.

Desert

The best way to build a desert shelter is to not build one. Locating the materials needed and building a shelter in the desert will consume vital water in the form of sweat. Living or dying

▲ During the heat of the day, shade is the best shelter in the desert.

in the desert often comes down to a matter of conserving sweat. Far better than building is to locate natural shelter: the shade of a large boulder or tree or a cave or recess of some kind.

Digging into the ground and covering it over with brush or a tarp if you have one, as recommended in some survival manuals, is only wise if you're remaining in one place, if you have a nearby source of water, and if there's no natural shade to be found. Otherwise, this requires too much expenditure of sweat.

An umbrella might not seem like critical survival gear, but it certainly can be in the desert.

Lacking an umbrella, make one by simply cutting a palm, as in the accompanying photo, or other branch. If the branch lacks enough leaves to shade you, drape your undershirt over it. With this field-expedient umbrella you have mobile shelter from the killing rays of desert sun. A few more palm fronds or branches will serve as nighttime shelter.

If the night is cold, as it is in some deserts at some times of the year, kindle a small fire near a boulder, if one is available, and sit between the fire and the boulder. If no boulder is available, and if it's very cold, proceed as we did

▲ An expedient umbrella: a fan palm frond.

with the cowboy who couldn't start a fire, adjusting for available fuel.

Alpine

The alpine environment above tree line is rock, snow, and ice. Alpine survival situations, ones in which people somehow find themselves above tree line without gear that would allow them to remain overnight safely, are unfortunately quite common. Skiers and snowboarders rarely carry any winter camping gear or survival gear or even a knife and a lighter. Many backpackers and backcountry climbers are equipped for only the best of conditions and unprepared for a mountain storm. Many backpackers don't even carry a knife, reasoning that they can open their packages of freeze-dried food with scissors. A backpacker, backcountry skier, or wilderness traveler of any kind without a good knife is like a paratrooper jumping without a reserve parachute.

The best survival strategy for a person above tree line is get down into the trees as soon as he or she is aware of a storm's approach. There you will find an environment rich with shelter and fire materials. Not being aware of

▲ Shelter framework ready for thatching with available material.

▲ Side view of partially built shelter, additional thatching and floor to be added.

weather to the extent that you are unaware of an approaching storm is not survival behavior.

The accompanying photos show one my students building an alpine shelter, his only tool being his fixed-blade knife. He first located a downed log to provide a base for his shelter. Then he built a framework with downed wood and green branches that he easily cut from a standing tree He placed a foot-thick layer of pine needles inside the shelter. Over the framework, which was left bare for photos, he will weave in more branches, and pile pine needles over them, at least a

foot thick. There is just enough room inside for him, and at the entrance just enough space for a tiny fire. Given that he is dressed for the climate, he could survive the night without a fire, relying only the insulation of the shelter in addition to his clothing. If he wants a fire, which he surely will, he will make a small stone fireplace and kindle a tiny fire. With this shelter and a fire, he could survive a blizzard in reasonable comfort. Construction time was fifty minutes.

This shelter was constructed in a relatively open area, using the scenario that the student wanted to be found by rescuers. Putting green pine needles on the fire would send up a smoke signal that could be seen for miles and aid rescuers in locating the survivor.

Temperate and Semi-Temperate Forest

Virtually any forest anywhere in the world provides abundant materials for building a survival shelter and for making a fire. During a weekend seminar three of my students, in a boreal rainforest in coastal Washington near the Canadian border, built a shelter with only folding knives. I provided no help other than instruction. They worked as a team. The most experienced member of the group selected a site with a thick standing tree as a base. Together they cut a supply of branches to build a framework. Then the experienced student constructed the framework while the others continued to cut branches and feed them to him. After the framework was constructed, they all gathered leaves and cut pine branches to cover the framework. They then stripped pine branches of offshoots and needles to make a thick insulating floor.

The temperature dropped and darkness fell as they worked. The light drizzle turned to sleet. The shutter of my camera froze and stopped working at about 15°F, judging by the thermometer on my jacket zipper. The shelter was complete in one hour and fifteen minutes, and was large enough for the four of us. With body heat alone, the inside temperature rose to 25°F above the ambient temperature.

After kindling a tiny fire about the size of my hat just inside the entrance with a flint-stick and knife, it grew so warm inside that we all removed our jackets. The sleet turned to snow around midnight. We continued to feed the tiny

fire. With the fire and our combined body heat it got so hot inside we stripped down to shirt-sleeves. Inside, the temperature rose to nearly 70°F. When we stepped outside into a foot of snow, my thermometer indicated 0°F.

This one-hour shelter was constructed in December and would serve during deepest winter. It stood as a teaching example for over a year with little modification. It was built in thick forest and with the scenario that the survivors did not want to be seen. Not one of my later students was able to find this shelter on their own, even after being told where in the general area it was located.

In the accompanying photo you can see a one-person demonstration nest I constructed in a fringe wilderness area in the foothills of the Stara Planina Mountains in Bulgaria. In this instance I used only a three- and one-half-inch blade fixed blade knife. First, I selected a tree to provide a base, then cut a waist-high stack of switches, which was the most available material. After arranging the switches to form walls, I tied them in place with vines, and thatched the outside with leaves and plant debris. I cut bundles of weeds and leaves to make a six-inch thick floor. A few rocks made a small fireplace, dead branches provided kindling and fuel. Due to having only the small knife, this nest required about an hour and a half to construct, longer than I like. I would have preferred to spend that extra time scouting for game. But I wanted to show my students that a small knife was workable. With a small fire, the shelter provided not only survival but comfort in temperatures that overnight dropped to well below freezing.

We deconstruct some shelters before moving on in order to leave no trace of our passing. In

▲ Winter "quickie shelter" made from gathered and available materials in Bulgaria.

this instance I let the shelter stand. It was still standing when I returned almost a year later in mid-winter. We cut some fresh pine boughs and added a layer to the outside and to the floor, gathered some wood, kindled a fire, and relaxed in comfort as we once again watched snow fall.

Semi-Tropic and Tropic

Building a mosquito-proof shelter in a tropical rainforest would be wonderful. Unfortunately, that's not possible in a survival situation unless you have a mosquito net in your pocket or your ready bag (and have that bag with you). To

▲ Shelter built from cut river cane.

deal with mosquitoes and other flying insects, you must rely on your clothing and a smudge (smoky) fire. Certain crushed leaves will serve as a natural repellent but without area expertise it's best to not try this, as you might easily rub your skin with poisonous leaves.

A shelter in the tropics will protect you from rain and keep you warm at night if necessary, depending on time of year, elevation, and area. Getting soaked can lead to hypothermia even in the tropics, especially if you're at high altitude. In a swampy area you'll want to construct a platform to keep you off the ground. In other areas, simply making a floor from available vegetation will do. I built the shelter in the photos as a demonstration for students. The scenario was that we were in an area with possible hostiles and inhabited by dangerous animals.

We quietly entered deep into a thickly forested secluded area near the mouth of a river. Taking note of available sign, I pointed out tracks of deer, a large cat, and many small animals, but no human tracks. Within that area I located a stand of river cane, a plant similar to bamboo. First, I made a large spear. This took two or three minutes. I decided to build the shelter inside the stand of river cane. Doing so would accomplish four things:

- Take advantage of the thick growth overhead, which meant I would not need to expend as much energy and time thatching the structure.
- All the materials were immediately at hand, so there was less energy expenditure and less movement was required.
- When complete, the shelter would be so unobtrusive that it could only be seen at very close range, and only by someone

directly in front of it. If need be, I could easily close off the front with a few more stalks of river cane.
- The thick stand of river cane combined with the structure of the shelter would provide security from approach by hostiles or predatory animals.

For instruction purposes, I alternated between two knives: a Fällkniven A1, an exceptionally well-designed, well-made, and well-balanced six-inch blade, and a Kellum Slasher, a light seven-inch blade. Both were capable of chopping. However, rather than chopping, which would make noise that could be heard at some distance, I press cut and carefully slashed the river cane. While I constructed the shelter, a student twenty yards away could hear nothing but the sound of rustling underbrush, which could be attributed to a large animal passing through or nesting.

Including flooring with river cane and leaves, the shelter required about forty-five minutes to construct. While cutting the river cane for the shelter, I stripped and set aside cane husks to be used as tinder, and some dead river cane for a small smokeless fire. In less than an hour I had a strong sharp spear, shelter, and the makings for fire. The immediate area was rich with game. The nearby river, a ten-minute slow stalk from the shelter, ran clear and was full of fish and crustaceans. If the area was secure (this was only a seminar) I could, using the small flint stick on my key ring, make a small smudge fire to keep mosquitoes away. If not secure, I could retreat inside my clothing like a turtle. I always wear comfortably loose clothing, whether I'm in the tropics and in a cold or temperate climate, city or bush, and have done so since I was issued my first set of jungle fatigues and found how much more comfortable and practical they were than tight-fitting jeans, shirts, and jackets. I no longer wear uniforms or camo, just loose and comfortable clothing.

With only a knife I had set up housekeeping without investing too much time or energy. If I wanted to move on at first light, I could do so without looking back and regretting all the work I had put into a dwelling. My chances of getting game at twilight when animals come to water were good. A fish spear, which would take another few minutes to make, would almost certainly provide fish. The two handkerchiefs I always carry would filter river water. The only thing lacking was a pot to boil water, and thereby disinfect it, and to make bug soup if unable to secure larger game. I could, however, boil water in a section of river cane, as you can with bamboo. Anyone with a good knife and good basic instruction could do the same. Having read this, perhaps you could too.

NOTE: If I had only a small fixed blade or survival folder, accomplishing the same thing would have taken two to three times as long. The river cane was tough. A small knife simply wouldn't have slashed through it with the same economy of effort. Still, I could have accomplished the same tasks.

Urban Shelter

In the event of earthquake, flood, or other natural disaster, or civil disturbance or pursuit by hostiles, you might find it necessary to seek or make shelter in an urban or semi-urban area. Abandoned buildings can serve this purpose, but you must exercise much caution in such

buildings. You can jimmy open a door with your knife, but might be taken for a criminal or looter if observed. Abandoned buildings can also have weak floors and roofs, especially after an earthquake, which could lead to injury. Long-abandoned buildings might also be home to bats, rats, and pigeons, all of which carry disease. Breathing dust from mouse or rat droppings or coming in contact with rodent urine, or being bitten, can cause infection with Hantavirus, a potentially fatal hemorrhagic fever. Bat and bird droppings contain Histoplasmosis, an infectious fungus that can be breathed in as dust and is often fatal.

Depending on the situation—only you can judge—you might do better to make shelter from urban debris or trash. As with wilderness shelter, think nest and make it small. Using your knife, you can cut cardboard to make a small tent-like shelter. If the shelter is just large enough for you to fit inside, and if you have an inch-thick layer of cardboard on the floor and walls, and if both ends are also closed with cardboard, the temperature inside can be as much as 25°F warmer than outside. Cutting foraged scraps of Styrofoam or similar materials and lining the interior of a cardboard tent will add considerable insulation. We have made cardboard tents with a one-inch thick lining of Styrofoam that, when occupied and heated only with body heat, was 55°F inside, when the ambient temperature was 27°F. Covering this sort of shelter with plastic bags can provide protection from rain and cold.

One of my correspondents, Mitchell, was in Peru during the 2007 earthquake. His hotel collapsed while he was out and he was left with only what he was wearing and what was in his day bag. In this instance his day bag was also his ready bag (as described in *The Tao of Survival* and in *Essential Survival Gear*) and it contained some essentials that proved critical. He could not get transportation to leave town. ATMs were down. He had little cash and no local contacts. He was in a mountain town and it was cold at night. Due to the quake, all was chaos.

Hundreds were killed in the initial shock. Despite warnings, many others were killed who went into damaged buildings after the initial shock. Survivors were dazed, and disoriented, many of them in shock. Others were deranged and became violent. Looters raided retail outlets and, in some cases, turned to robbery.

Mitchell made camp in a public park, an open area where there was no danger of buildings collapsing, and sheltered by bushes so that his camp was not visible to casual passersby. With his knife, he ripped fiberglass sheets from the side of a damaged market building to use as roof and walls. He then cut up cardboard boxes and Styrofoam padding from boxes used to ship electronics. With Duct tape from his bag, he taped that material to the interior walls. He took a backseat from an abandoned auto as a bed. Reaching through the broken windows and semi-crushed window frames of his hotel, he cut sections of thick curtains to use for blankets. This shelter allowed him to sleep warm and get enough rest to better cope with the situation.

Mitchell helped others, advising them to not try to return to their houses until the danger of secondary shocks had passed, showing them how to make emergency shelters, providing emergency medical help and salvaged food and bottled water from the public market. Once three men attempted to rob him—he looked like what he was, a rich foreigner—but backed down when he responded aggressively with the large knife from his ready bag. Relief attempts during the first week were chaotic and ineffective. Help did eventually come, transportation was restored, and Mitchell was able to continue his journey.

This kind of thing could happen to anyone anywhere—including you. The aftermath of Hurricane Katrina was much worse than the earthquake in Peru, as was the 2011 earthquake and tsunami that devastated Japan and damaged the Fukushima nuclear plant, and the 2004 Indian Ocean earthquake and tsunami that resulted in the deaths of more than 250,000 people in over a dozen countries. Survivors of all these disasters had to make do with whatever they could make or find for shelter and for food and water, sometimes for weeks.

Scrap sheet metal and corrugated fiberglass, scrap plywood, tarpaper, cardboard, plastic sheeting, polystyrene, and similar materials are often strewn about and available after a disaster. All can be used to construct an emergency shelter. Such materials used to build larger shelters, combined with something on the order of a hobo stove for heat and cooking, and a water bucket for plumbing, are in fact home to millions of people in developing nations. In some instances, these dwellings have served their builders better than concrete buildings that collapsed during an earthquake. Actually, owner-built homes of this nature, although some might think of them as shacks or survival hovels, are home to the majority of the people now living on Earth. The people who live in them built them because they had no place else to live, no money, and little choice. These people are true survivors.

Clothing and Foraged Shelter

Clothing is your first line of defense and should be appropriate for the climate. Detailed information on simple, minimal, survival-appropriate clothing suitable for all but formal occasions is in *Essential Survival Gear*. If your clothing is inadequately insulated, you can supplement it with other materials, and by using your knife to cut field grass or fresh leaves from tree branches (dry leaves crumble and those on the ground are usually wet) and stuff them between your inner and outer garments to provide additional insulation. Scavenged cardboard, newspaper, Styrofoam pieces, bubble wrap, and similar materials cut to size, can serve as well. For this to be effective, your clothing should fit loosely.

In the desert or while trekking on an uninhabited beach, cutting a palm frond or a bare branch and spreading your undershirt over it creates field-expedient umbrella that could save you from heatstroke and serious sunburn. Loose-fitting cotton or linen clothing can be wetted to provide evaporative cooling in arid environments and can be your best protection from heatstroke in any hot environment. The simplest shelter from a tropical rain, which when accompanied by wind can turn cold, is to cut a large leaf from, say, a banana tree and use it as an umbrella. Those same banana leaves or palm fronds can become part of a nighttime shelter.

In our highly technological and specialized society, few of us consider that many objects and materials can be used as raw materials to make lifesaving shelter. All you need is a simple tool and some ingenuity. Thinking about the immediate situation, reviewing basic principles, and being creative, is using a survivor's mindset.

Escaping a Building on Fire or Damaged by Earthquake

A survival knife can be an aid in escaping a building that's on fire, or one that has been damaged by an earthquake. Your first line of defense is of course your awareness of danger, your analysis of the danger, and your decision on how to act.

If you're on the first floor of a burning building and far from a door, you might simply jump out of a nearby window—or you might elect to help others. If you're on an upper floor of a high rise and trapped inside by a locked door, your knife could be instrumental in saving your life and that of others. This happened to me once. I recounted the story in *The Tactical Knife*. In short, I used my fixed blade, a Randall Model, and a woman's platform shoe as a baton, to cut through a locked fire door. In actual method it wasn't much different than batoning wood, a skill described earlier in this book.

Many years ago, one of my friends was asleep in his room on an upper floor of a hotel when he was awakened by smoke and fire. Using his pocketknife, he quickly cut the heavy king-sized bedspread into a manageable size and soaked it in the shower. He then crawled down the smoke-filled corridor to the fire stairs, all the while keeping under most of the smoke and using the section of wet bedspread as a cape and breathing filter. Wrapping the bedspread around himself, he was able to exit the hotel without being burned or suffering smoke inhalation.

As every resident of California knows, you need to get outside at the first tremor of an earthquake—if possible. If you cannot get outside, and you find yourself trapped in a semi-collapsed building, a survival knife could help to save your life by using it as digging tool. The trick to doing so is to find a point of little resistance and use your blade to weaken it, and to then remove building materials, carefully.

Mortar will give way to a blade, as will concrete, albeit at the cost of damage to your blade, which would be a minor concern if you were so trapped. However, using the spine of your blade and pressing and scraping rather than stabbing and slashing will be more effective and will better preserve your blade, your escape tool.

▲ Fred Perrin Mid Tech Bowie being used to deconstruct a stone wall.

Chapter Seven

Field-Expedient Tool and Weapon Making

When crafting tools such as spears, throwing sticks, and bows and arrows, the difference in efficiency between the small knife and medium knife is as marked as it is in shelter building, and as significant. For example, using the right technique, you can cut a wrist-sized sapling of softwood with a small blade in a minute or two. Hardwood will require a multiple of that time, say, four to five minutes. Smoothing a spear shaft and sharpening a spear point with the small knife will require about ten minutes with softwood and double that with hardwood. Since hardwood makes a better spear, you should use hardwood if it's available. So, let's say it takes you twenty minutes to make a good functional spear with a small knife. This is about the average amount of time required by a reasonably proficient beginning student.

A properly designed and constructed medium-sized knife enables the same student to chop through that wrist-sized sapling in four strokes, which requires only seconds and provides a rough point to start with. Then, when you sharpen the point, instead of carving you can chop and slash a functional point in a few more seconds. If you want a finer point, carving will be easier with the larger knife because you have more weight and power behind the edge. Smoothing the shaft is done by simply running the edge down the shaft and cutting through small branches at their base. The average time expended amounts to about five minutes total. Time saved is calories saved.

A few hours work with a well-designed small knife and an equally well-designed medium-sized knife will demonstrate the greater efficiency of the larger knife for all tasks except intricate carving. This should be taken into account not only when selecting a survival knife but in planning the work to be done.

The Spear

I regard the spear as the primary primitive weapon/tool for the survivor and the first weapon/tool that should be crafted, for the following reasons:

- Spears are quick and easy to make.
- Spears extend your reach, and with a simple thrust allow you to take small animals: everything from lizards, frogs, snakes, and fish to small mammals, without exposing yourself to being bitten or clawed.
- A strong spear thrust will even allow the taking of large mammals, also without exposing yourself to horn or hoof—if you have the other skills required to do so.
- A lightweight spear or javelin can be thrown to take an animal at some distance and/or while it's moving.
- A spear provides significant protection from hostile wildlife such as feral dogs, big cats, wild boar, and even aggressive bears. Also, there are hostile humans in this world.

In these days of smart phones and laptops, of digital games and the Internet, most of us are

▲ Spear made from an oak sapling.

far from our own roots as primeval hunters. And so the spear might seem incredibly primitive, or even ridiculous, as a weapon for a survivor. It is not. There are many modern examples of spear hunters.

Alexander "Sasha" Siemel was internationally famous from the 1930s through the 1950s, and well known until his death in 1970, as a hunter of jaguar in Brazil. He hunted jaguars with a spear to protect livestock and villagers during a time when jaguars were considered a menace and often killed farmers and their children. He learned to use a spear and his hunting methods from a local Indian. Siemel wrote that hunting big cats with a spear was in some ways safer than with a gun, in that the jaguars always charged and a strong spear was more certain to stop them than a bullet.

Still today, in the twenty-first century, each year French hunters on foot take wild boar, *sanglier*, with the spear. This ancient weapon and method of hunting is now spreading to other counties in Europe, and is also practiced in some states in the US. Siemel used, and the European spear hunters also usually use, dogs in the chase. Few native hunters do. Like the Masai of Africa do, you can even take a lion with a spear, if you have the other necessary requirements to face and kill a lion with a primitive weapon. Not that you'd want to kill a lion, given that they've lost 80 percent of their habitat and are in danger of extinction. Just saying. A spear can be a formidable weapon.

Inspired by reading, I taught myself to make and use the spear at a very early age. By the time I was twelve I had taken a fair amount of small game in my area with a spear. Later, in my twenties, after military service and survival training, and after reading about Sasha Siemel

and his exploits, I fashioned heavy-duty spears and took larger animals with them. With some practice, the spear is a perfectly viable hunting weapon.

On the subject of self-protection in the wild, there are many who say that there are no wild creatures that would attack a human without provocation in North America or Europe. To those folks I would say—you haven't spent enough time in wilderness, or in areas where human housing overlaps the natural habitat of predators. Cougars do attack humans, as do packs of feral dogs, and bears, and moose, in the US, Canada, and Europe. Coyote packs, usually considered harmless to humans, usually are harmless. But there has been more than one instance where a coyote pack has attacked a small child or an injured adult. A cursory scan of the news will find many instances of adults being attacked by cougars in Canada and states such as California and Colorado. Most cougar victims were severely injured. Some were killed.

I was once charged by an angry wild boar the size of a Volkswagen in the Central Massif of France. While walking along a trail with a small rucksack, minding my own business, not hunting or in any way bothering the creature, except perhaps by my presence, he crashed out of the brush onto the trail behind me. I had felt his presence and heard him coming but thought little of it. I knew there were many boars in the area but so far none had bothered me. He looked at me with what was clearly a bad attitude, snorted, and took a couple of steps in my direction. I experienced a moment of surprise, as wild boar always run away, or so I thought, then made for a nearby tree as he got off the mark. I levitated to a low-hanging branch where I stayed for fifteen or twenty minutes while Sir Swine snorted and dug at the base of the tree with his formidable tusks. Although domestic pigs in France are used to find truffles and dig them up, I doubt this fellow was seeking the fragrant fungus. Eventually he got tired or bored and wandered off. This story would have turned out differently if no climbable tree had been close. A few days later, a local friend, one of the guys who hunt boar with a spear, told me there were a few bad-tempered boar in those woods and that they would attack you. He never went there alone without a gun or his spear. I haven't returned to that forest since then without being armed, preferably with a firearm or spear but at least with a large knife.

Two of my sons were stalked by cougars in California, a state where cougars are protected and where their habitat has been overrun by development. They were twelve and eight at the time. We were backpacking in the Los Padres Wilderness in Southern California. The boys encountered a cougar while gathering firewood about fifty yards from camp. They escaped being mauled and possibly killed by doing what they were taught from an early age.

First and most important, they were tuned into their environment. This enabled them to become aware of the big cat as it crouched in the underbrush before it attacked. The older and larger boy faced the cat with a large tomahawk in hand, not a weapon of choice but what he had available as he was using it to chop wood. The smaller boy moved to the rear of the larger one. Rather than running, which would have triggered an attack, they walked backwards slowly and carefully, moving together, the larger boy keeping his eyes on the cat, the smaller one looking to the rear

for secure footing. They shouted loudly in an attempt to frighten the cat, and to call for help. In this way they got close enough to camp for me to hear them.

I ran to them and escorted them back to camp. I could have shot the cougar with my handgun, but didn't want to kill it if not absolutely necessary. The big cat, it looked to be about one hundred and sixty pounds, followed us to our fire, stalking us the same way a house cat will stalk a mouse. It was not scared away by our campfire, or by our shouting and banging pots and pans—measures often recommended by "experts." My brother-in-law and I took turns on watch, as the cougar circled our camp until near dawn, when it finally disappeared. A wildlife biologist later told me that cougars get prey fixation and often will stalk a child, a pet, or an adult, for days. I later read of cases where this happened in suburban areas near cougar habitat, the cougar eventually coming over a fence and into a yard to take a pet or child.

That said, I do not mean to overstate the dangers of wild animals. The North American wilderness is not especially dangerous in regard to wild animals and should not be entered with anxiety. Awareness of your surroundings will result in increased enjoyment of the wild as well as alert you to possible dangers and increase the odds of your survival in critical situations. Of course it is well known that if you find yourself in a wilderness survival situation in some areas of the world—Latin America, Africa, and parts of Asia and Eastern Europe, for example—there are many animals prepared and perfectly willing to dispute the proposition that humans are at the top of the food chain.

The Staff

Some survival books recommend a staff as the first survival weapon/tool to make. The reasoning is that with a staff you have a tool that will aid you in crossing shallow streams, or perhaps aid you in climbing or descending a hill, and will function as an impact weapon, one that can be used to fend off angry or feral dogs. I view a staff as a spear without a point, and think it is very useful, particularly in built-up semi-rural areas, or in fringe primitive areas such as exist in many developing nations where villages are at the edge of wilderness. In those instances, a staff is less threatening to friendly folks than a spear and can quickly be converted to a spear with your knife, if the need arises.

In the Balkans, Russia, some Eastern European countries, India, Asia, parts of Latin America, and other places, feral dog packs are common and dangerous. Bulgaria, for example, has the largest population of European jackals, which interbreed with feral dogs, and is plagued with such attacks. These packs attack frequently, and sometimes kill. During a period of five years when I was spending a good bit of time in the Balkans I was attacked three times by dog/jackal packs either in or near villages. On two occasions I was able to fight them off with walking staff and rocks. On the other occasion I had only my knife. There were only four dogs in this pack (as opposed to six and more than a dozen in the other two attacked). On this occasion I was able to get my back to a wall and injure the alpha enough to make him retreat; more about that attack and defensive tactics in the chapter on self-defense. The other dogs in that pack retreated with the alpha. Such attacks are not uncommon, even in the capitol

city, Sofia, where an American was killed by a feral dog pack two years ago. A British woman who I know was attacked a few months ago and suffered many wounds before a passerby could beat off the dogs with a stick. Yet another woman was killed by dogs in a village near the one we were visiting. In a rural area, the staff is innocuous and good to have. In wilderness, I prefer to make and carry a spear.

How to Make a Spear

A quickly made spear can save your life, not only in wilderness, but in areas where you might encounter packs of feral dogs, and in disaster zones where you might encounter feral humans and need a defensive weapon that will keep some distance between yourself and assailants who do not have firearms.

Making a spear is simplicity itself. Select a reasonably straight sapling about as tall as you are; a few inches taller than your head is okay. A thin shaft, about an inch in diameter, is best for a throwing spear. A thicker shaft, an inch and one half to two inches in diameter, is generally better for a thrusting spear. The thickness of the shaft should be according to the area and your needs.

In the desert, where you will mostly find small creatures, and are unlikely to find a tall straight sapling of any kind, you need only a shaft about an inch or so in diameter for both throwing and thrusting. Yes, there are bighorn sheep and other large mammals in some deserts, but they are few and difficult to approach. If you can get close enough to spear one, they can be taken with a thin spear if thrown powerfully and accurately. Aborigines take kangaroos of the Australian desert with relatively thin spears as a matter of course. I have personally taken animals of similar size with a thin spear or javelin thrown powerfully at close range. In woodland, jungle, estuary, veldt, or other environments where thicker shafts are available, and where you are more likely to encounter larger animals, and perhaps more dangerous animals, the thicker shaft is better. But there are no hard and fast rules on spear shaft thickness. You will have to judge this for yourself according to available materials and game and the terrain.

Hardwood makes a stronger spear than softwood, but serviceable spears can be made from just about any wood, including pine and willow, which are quite soft. Bamboo and river cane, both technically grasses, make excellent spears. Both are easy to cut and sharpen, yet take a sharp, tough point.

Cut the shaft near the base of the sapling. If you use a downward press cut or chop, you'll make the next step easier. Sharpen a point at this end. Trim off all protrusions and smooth the shaft. Trim the butt so it is rounded. That's it. You now have a functional spear. Later, if you wish, you can harden the point by heating over hot coals (not fire, which would burn it). The point will also naturally harden, as will the entire shaft, as time passes and the wood dries

▲ Fishing spear made using Mykel Hawke's Peregrine.

and becomes seasoned. If you want, and if you have the time and resources, you can also craft a sharp tough point from bone (or stone if you have flintknapping skills) and lash it to the tip of your shaft.

Do not tie your knife to the shaft to make a spear. Many survival manuals advise doing this, but it is unnecessary and can lead to damage or loss of your most important tool. Remember, your knife is your primary tool and is to be used to make other tools.

To make a multi-point spear for fishing, simply split the tip into four or more sections, place a wedge at the base of the splits to hold them open, or lash them open, and sharpen the individual points. Some advocate the multi-point spear for taking small mammals. I do not. The split points will impede penetration and should not be used for anything other than fish, amphibians, lizards, and snakes. Also, if used on land, the smaller and more fragile points will easily break, thus rendering your spear useless and requiring you to make another.

How to Use a Spear

To take an animal by thrusting, or even throwing, with a spear, you must first, obviously, get within range of the creature. If your senses are fully engaged and you are blending with your immediate environment, you can accomplish this, although it will likely take some practice (as I describe in another section).

Small game animals, and sometimes even large game animals, are often encountered when you're simply walking toward your destination—again, if you are alert and blending with your environment—and can be taken by a quick response. Spotting animal tracks, a rabbit or deer run, an area dug up by boar, nut shells with tooth marks, droppings, and so on, which you are likely to do if your senses are engaged, will give you an indication of what animals are in the area. If you locate such signs, and if you think it's more important to get food than to continue to cover ground, selecting a place near a game trail or water source to rest quietly and watch for game to pass by might well get you close enough to make a telling throw or thrust. Stalking might be more effective if you're able to move quietly and with awareness of wind and other movements in your area. Only you will be able to determine your best approach according to your abilities and the immediate environment.

To take large game with a thrust, you will need to take a strong stance and firmly brace your shaft using both hands. You must strike quickly and powerfully. Most likely you will need to rush in explosively from concealment to get close enough for an effective thrust. Practicing this before need is a very good thing to do. Once you have thrust a spear into a large animal, back off and stay away from the animal until it expires. It is unlikely that a single spear thrust will result in immediate death. The animal will struggle and you could be injured if you are too close. More than one thrust might be necessary but do not attempt another thrust, or thrusts, until the animal is near death and helpless. All this may sound cruel, and in fact it is. Survival hunting is not sport hunting. Small animals may be taken with a one-handed thrust.

The best way to throw a spear is to hold the shaft at the balance point, bring it back over your shoulder, and, while focusing on a vital point on your target, throw it directly over your shoulder in a straight line—similar to throwing a dart. You will impart much more force to your throw if you begin by standing sideways to your target, then forcefully turn your shoulders and hips toward the target as you throw and release.

To successfully take fish with a spear, move the point slowly toward the fish and under the surface of the water until the tips of the spear are quite close to your target. Then thrust quickly and smoothly.

Walkabout

If you would like to see spears used to opportunistically take game while on the move, watch the movie, *Walkabout*. The aboriginal boy in the film, David Gulpilil, was not an actor at the time of filming. The scenes where he is spearing everything from lizards to kangaroos were not staged and clearly show how effective the spear is as a survivor's hunting weapon. He also uses a throwing stick/club.

A spear will give you vital distance from your prey and, in doing so, help to protect you from its teeth and claws. But, you might get hurt. Even a rabbit has teeth and will bite and scratch to try to save its life. A larger animal, say a raccoon, will fight you harder and with more strength and speed that you might imagine if you haven't had experience with wild creatures. Pound for pound wild animals are stronger and faster than humans. Do not even consider taking on a larger animal until you have some experience with smaller ones unless you are desperate and have no other choice. Even deer, Bambi-eyed, cute, lovable

deer, have sharp hooves and horns and teeth. They can and will use those weapons to defend themselves, as many hunters have found to their dismay when they approached downed deer they thought were dead but which were only wounded. Wild boar are ill tempered and powerful, have tusks and sharp hooves, and can knock you off your feet before you realize their intention. Most of them, most of the time, will try to run away, but if you've got a spear stuck in one of them, you're in for a fight. Often, the best strategy for taking a large animal is to strike as deeply as you can and then back off and wait for it to weaken and track it as it tries to escape. You'll have to judge the situation for yourself.

Smaller creatures are more plentiful, easier to approach, safer to try and take, and should be the survivor's first choice for prey. After you have some experience with smaller animals, including fish, lizards, amphibians, and non-poisonous snakes, and you've committed to the process, you might want to try for larger game. Or not. In most environments a survivor can get by for extended periods by hunting only small animals. You will find that practicing on inanimate targets before going after game will be of great benefit.

The Atlatl—An Accessory to the Spear

Atlatl is a *Nahuatl* (Aztec) word that has become common usage for spear throwers, a tool that uses leverage to achieve greater velocity and power in spear throwing. Australian aborigines call the same device a *woomera*, and in remote regions still use it today. The atlatl has been in widespread usage in many societies around the world from the Paleolithic period through the ancient Greeks to more recent history, when

Native Americans met the firearms of Spanish invaders with atlatls and darts

The atlatl enables a thin spear, or dart, or javelin—different names, same thing—to be thrown with greater velocity and force than can be achieved by muscle power alone. It is a deceptively simple device, essentially a lever, easy to make, and not difficult to use. I was first introduced to the atlatl at a gathering of people interested in primitive technology. As a spear user since childhood, I immediately saw the atlatl's value. I made my first atlatl in about a half hour, and with about twenty minutes of practice was able to cast a dart with reasonable accuracy and considerable force to about thirty yards, much farther than I could throw a spear with force and accuracy without it. You can do the same. My son, who was ten at the time, did so.

To make an atlatl, first select a stick about as long as your forearm, or a little longer, that has a knot, or protrusion, at one end. If you cannot locate such a stick, find a forked sapling and carve the fork into the shape needed, or carve into a shaft to create a protrusion at one end. The knob on your atlatl will fit into a socket at the butt of your spear. Alternately, carve a socket into the atlatl and fit the butt of the dart into the socket. Either will work.

To use the atlatl, fit the knob or socket to the butt of your spear, and hold the atlatl parallel with the spear. Hold the spear with your forefinger and thumb. The atlatl rests on your palm and is grasped with your other fingers. Begin your throw as previously described. At the moment of release, let go of the shaft and retain hold on the atlatl. If you've been practicing spear throwing, you'll probably find that you hit close to your target. A few hours of practice will allow you to achieve survival level proficiency.

The Throwing Stick

The second primitive weapon to make with your knife and add to your survivor's armory is the throwing stick, sometimes called a rabbit stick for its frequent use for just that purpose—taking rabbits. However, the throwing stick can be effective on larger animals as well as rabbits. A strong, well-placed throw can knock a deer or other sizable animal senseless and allow the hunter to rush in and complete the kill with his spear—or to beat it to death with the throwing stick, an ugly but sometimes necessary act. The throwing stick can also be used as an impact weapon—a club—without being thrown. In this instance the survivor might anchor a large reptile or small animal with his spear, then finish the kill with the throwing stick used as a club. I regard both the spear and throwing stick as essential survival weapons and tools. They work well together and have complimentary functions.

A throwing stick is simply a stick about the diameter of your wrist, or smaller, and about two feet in length. A curved stick throws better and more accurately than a straight one. Often the stick is planed flat on its lateral surfaces. If done with craft and care, it becomes a boomerang. The hunting boomerang is not designed to return, as are the ones made for play. The flat planes help to stabilizes the stick in flight and make a narrower striking surface, which transmits more force to a smaller area on impact.

How to Make a Throwing Stick

Locate a suitable length of wood, which can be the branch of a standing tree or downed wood.

▲ A finished and planed rabbit stick is on the left. The one on the right is a rough and ready rabbit stick, which can be used as it is.

Cut or chop it to length. You can now use it as it is. I always prefer to strip the bark and carve a comfortable handle so that the release, when throwing, is smoother and the grip more comfortable when used as a club. To make a throwing stick that will fly better, plane down the two surfaces that will be parallel when the stick is oriented sideway to the ground.

How to Use a Throwing Stick

Basically, you throw the stick as you would a baseball by, if possible, standing sideways to the target, then turning your shoulders and hips toward the target as you release the stick. Sight your target and focus tightly on the spot you wish to hit. In an open area, throw the stick with a sidearm throw so that it spins parallel to the ground. This spin creates a projectile that has a striking area two feet in diameter and imparts a great deal of force to the stick through centrifugal action, especially at its tips. In an area such as a forest with many trees, throw the stick vertically so that it is less likely to hit a tree or branch before impacting your target. The use of a stick for a club is, I think, obvious, and brutal—though sometimes necessary.

The Survival Bow

Although the bow can cast an arrow farther than anyone can throw a spear or throwing stick (the exception being darts thrown with an atlatl) and therefore take game at longer ranges, I place it lower in survival importance than either one because:

- Bow construction is much more complex than that of simpler weapons.
- Bows require much more time to build.

- All the required materials may not be available.
- The bow is in essence a system, rather than a stand-alone weapon, in that is has three separate components: bow, string, and arrow; and the arrow which, if it is to be accurate at long range, must have yet another component, fletching, usually made from feathers, and thus requires even more components: glue or cordage, or both, to adhere the fletching to the arrows.

That said, if the materials are readily available and the investment of time worthwhile, the survivor might want to craft a bow and arrows, depending on the immediate situation, how much time is available, and how much the survivor needs to extend his reach. The survival bow is not a fine piece of craftsmanship, as are many handmade bows. Nor does it have the dependability and function of one of today's factory-made bows. However, I've hunted game successfully with what amounted to survival bows as a boy and later as an adult with native hunters in Latin America and Asia. Many others have also done so, as these skills are not unique. The survival bow is one that can be made fairly quickly and will work reasonably well. It may well be rough and ugly compared to the handsome commercial bows you might have seen. It can, however, kill, and aid survival.

How to Make a Survival Bow

Yew and osage orange are top choices of bowyers, but hickory, elm, ash, juniper, choke cherry, and almost any fruit wood can be used to make an excellent bow. Birch, pine, and eucalyptus, while not satisfactory for the professional archer, will also do fine for a survival bow. Actually, there are far too many kinds of wood that can be used for a bow to try and list them here. Any reasonably springy and strong wood can be used.

Try a few different kinds of wood, whatever is growing in your immediate area, by bending a few saplings of about two inches in diameter and seeing if they spring back to their original shape. If you find a sapling that seems both springy and strong, cut it off near its base. It does not have to be perfectly straight; about three to four feet is a good length. Longer will make for a smoother release and arrow cast but will be more difficult to maneuver in woods and brush.

Based on the balance point of the wood, select the center and find the natural curve if any. The part of the bow that faces away from you is the back. The side that faces you is the belly. If the sapling has a slight natural curve, work with it and make the concave side the belly. After marking off a short section for the handle—say about five inches—cut the limbs to about equal length. Then, cutting away from the handle, first on one limb and then on the other, carve away the wood on the belly. Continue until the belly is fairly flat. Leave the handle full thickness.

Be careful to not cut too deeply into the belly, as this will ruin the wood and you'll have to start over. As you carve the belly, bend the stave a little to see that it bends without making any sign that it will break. Do not yet bend it more than about twenty degrees. The wood is still green and will need to set for a while—at least a day in a dry climate—so that it will bend and spring back to shape without breaking.

When the belly is more or less flat and about a half-inch thick, stop carving. Now turn your edge perpendicular to the belly and scrape away the rest of the wood to be removed. When it seems like you've reached a point where the bow that is now taking shape will still require a fairly strong pull to draw but is not so thin that it will break, stop scraping.

The belly should be as smooth and flat as you can make it. The back can be left as it is, as there is no need to even remove the bark. The limbs of the bow, the parts that extend each side from the handle, might be a little crooked or have

▲ Three survival bows: (left) a quickie bow made from eucalyptus, (middle) a bow made from willow, (right) a bow made from choke cherry.

irregularities. This is not important. Leave them in place. Notch each limb about an inch from the end where you will secure the bowstring. Now set the bow aside for a while, at least overnight.

> **NOTE:** If you're pushed for time you can make a survival bow by simply cutting a springy sapling to a useful length and foregoing any carving. Given that you've selected good wood the resulting bow will be functional.

In the sixties, I hunted the Yucatan jungle with Lacandon Indians, members of a Mayan ethnic group living in southern Mexico and northern Guatemala. Their bows were plain shafts with no carving. The belly of each bow was simply the side of the sapling that was naturally concave. Their arrows were made of cane with hardwood fore shafts and stone points and were almost as long as their bows. The lengthy arrow, after penetrating an animal, protruded from the wound and impeded the animal's escape in thick undergrowth. The bows were weak and the arrows did not fly very fast or far. Shots were taken only at very close range, often up into tree branches where many small animals lived. A well-known experimental archeologist, a good friend, told me that the Lacandon had previously made more sophisticated archery equipment. That may well be true. It's also true that the Lacandon, who could afford single-shot .22 rifles, used them in

▲ Lacandon bow and arrows.

preference to any bow. The Lacandon I hunted with were not by any definition good hunters but managed to obtain some food. I was successful with the same equipment. More on that in *A Story of The Tao of The Hunt*, which follows.

Aboriginal peoples used many types of bows and have continued to use them even into modern times to take game, adapting their gear as needed according to the environment and available materials. The photo on the previous page shows a bow, bow case, and arrows I got from indigenous people I hunted with in Indonesia. The areas we hunted varied from thick jungle to open terrain. The archery equipment reflects this in that it's suitable for varied terrain. The bow limbs are quite strong. The arrows are thin, light, fly very fast, and are tipped with scavenged sheet metal. The entire outfit is compact and lightweight, well suited to the environment, the available game, and people of small stature.

Both of these groups used their bows to take fish and amphibians, as well as any and all land animals. Adjust the equipment you make as appropriate to local conditions, and according to available materials, and practice the hunting methods outlined in another section of this book, and you too can survive with primitive tools and weapons—if you have a knife with which to make them. Lacking a knife, you would have to first make stone tools, a specialized topic covered in some of the books I recommend.

How to Make a Bowstring for your Survival Bow

Making an effective bowstring will require a tough material, such as palm fiber, animal (or

◄ Twisting fibers together to make a bow string for the survival bow.

human) hair, or other tough plant material. If you've already killed any animal with your other weapons, or found a dead one, you can make a superior bowstring from twisted sinew or strips of skin. You can also use a shoelace, or cut thin strips from, say, your shirt, and braid them together. Finding the right material for a bowstring is often the most difficult part of making a survival bow. For this and other reasons I always have a short length of strong thin cord in a pocket whenever I'm in the wilderness. I also carry dental floss, which can be braided to make a bowstring.

How to Make Survival Arrows

Most any straight or mostly straight shoot will do. Birch, willow, cane, reed, and bamboo all make good arrows, but any straight, stiff shoot will be good enough for a survival arrow. Cut them to about half the length of the bow or a little less. Scrape off all bark, knots, rough places, and make the shaft as smooth as possible. Heating the shaft over hot coals, not fire, will warm it and help to bend any curves to make them straight.

Carve a notch in the end where the string will go. Sharpen the point. An ordinary sharp shaft

▲ The bottom arrow is highly finished with fletching and stone arrowhead, middle and top are works in progress, but can be used as is at close range.

without a stone or bone point will do to bring down small game. Let the arrow shafts lay flat at least overnight to dry. If they take on a curve while drying, heat and bend straight. Three arrows are sufficient for the survival hunter.

If you intend to try for game any larger than, say, a raccoon, it's best to make a point that will make a larger and deeper wound channel than the sharpened shaft. Arrowheads can be carved with your knife from bone or hard wood, or cut from scavenged tin cans or metal scraps. You can also knap (chip) an arrowhead from stone, a discarded glass bottle, or window glass. Describing that skill is beyond the parameters of this book. If you want to learn flint knapping, please refer to the books suggested.

Arrowheads need to be set into a notch at the point and lashed in place. Almost any thin plant can serve for this purpose—see cordage—but animal sinew is better. If you first take a rabbit, squirrel, or other animal with your spear or throwing stick, you'll have an adequate source of sinew.

How to Make Fletching for Your Survival Bow

An arrow without fletching will serve for short ranges, but if you release a few un-fletched

▲ These feathers could be used for fletching an arrow.

arrows, you will find their limits. To add fletching, you need feathers or possibly tough leaves such as palm. Feathers can often be found on the ground as you pass through areas where birds live. Failing that, look for bird's nests. Feathers can often be found on the ground nearby. Or, you can take a bird, thereby obtaining plenty of feathers, plus a meal. Sitting birds are relatively easy to take with a throwing stick.

Making fletching is a fiddly task requiring patience and nimble fingers. First split the spine of the feather with your knife. Then cut the split sections of feathers to length for vanes; about three inches is good, four is better if the feathers are long enough. You will need three vanes and a means of attaching them to the arrow.

Pine sap or resin will do, as will other sticky tree saps. You will also need some very thin fiber to lash the vanes in place. The fiber can be stripped from many plants or you can use sinew, which is better, if you have any. Dental floss will also work very well. First glue the vanes in place, then lash them. If you have no glue of any kind, vanes can be lashed in place without it. Attach the first vane parallel with the arrowhead. Attach the other two equidistant from the first. The simplest way to apply the lashing is to first wrap the fiber around the base of the arrow and the vanes close to the nock. Then do the same to the forward ends of the vanes. After the vanes are attached carefully, cut off the portion of the spine protruding from the lashing so that it doesn't catch on the bow when released.

How to Use a Survival Bow

Everyone knows that you fit the nock of an arrow to the bowstring, pull it back, and release

◀ Drawing the bow using a survival arrow.

©ML Ayres

it, right? The most common method of doing this is called the Mediterranean draw. To use this method, place your forefinger on the string above the arrow, and your middle and ring finger below it. If you are right handed, the arrow goes on the left of the bow; if left handed, on the right. Lightly hold the arrow between your forefinger and middle finger. Pull the arrow back toward your cheek while pushing on the bow with your other hand. Release the string and arrow as smoothing as possible when the bow comes to full draw. You will be able to feel when it reaches full draw by directing your attention to the bow and how it feels.

There are other methods of drawing the bow, including the pinch draw, which is not especially effective with a strong bow, and the Mongolian draw, which I prefer. For the Mongolian draw you anchor the string in the first joint of your thumb and secure the tip of your thumb with your forefinger. Release by letting your finger slip from your thumb. To hit your target, keep your eyes and your attention focused on a small part of the target, such as the shoulder of a rabbit. Do not shoot at the whole animal. When you release, your arrow does so smoothly.

Digging Sticks

Digging sticks are made by sharpening any stick sturdy enough to dig with. A flat chisel- or shovel-like point will serve better than a sharp spear-like point. They are used to dig up edible roots and tubers, which provide a good source of carbohydrates. A good complete survival manual, or a field guide to plants, will help you to identify edible tubers and other plants.

Ninety percent of wild plants are inedible and a significant percentage of them are poisonous. Many edible wild plants have poisonous look-a-likes that grow near them. If you cannot precisely identify a plant, do not eat it. In doubt, use the edible plant test in the books I recommend, but even then, do not risk eating a plant you are not sure of.

NOTE: Edible plants are not required to sustain life.

Cordage

You can make cordage simply by twisting or braiding almost any plant fiber. By experimenting with different plants in your area, you will find which are stronger. Palm fiber, willow, and other barks, and many stems, can be stripped with your knife to produce fiber. Once you have fiber, twist it into cordage, joining sections by splicing them together to make them longer. Twisted cordage can be braided to make thick, strong rope. If the fibers are too dry to twist or braid, wet them until they are soft enough, then let them dry in place after twisting or braiding.

▲ Cordage stripped from palm spines.

Animal sinew makes excellent cordage. Strip it from the bones of whatever animal you have taken and let it dry to keep it. Sinew must be moistened to make cordage; when it dries in place, it will be very strong. Thin strips of animal skin can also be twisted or braided to make cordage.

Containers

If you need to carry water and don't have a folded plastic bag or condom in your pocket, you can make one from an animal skin. Remove the hind feet with your knife, and cut a slit from ankle to ankle. Then peel off the skin in a one-piece tube. Instruction in tanning is beyond the scope of this book, but the skin can be used by scraping away tissue down to the skin and letting it dry in the sun. Collecting containers for berries and nuts can be made from the bark of various trees, but in a survival situation they usually aren't worth the trouble. Berries and nuts can easily be collected in a handkerchief or shirt.

▲ Berries and acorns collected in a handkerchief.

Chapter Eight

Hunting and Foraging with Primitive Weapons and Tools

Tuning In and Blending with Your Environment

Since the focus of this book is the survival knife and its uses, I cannot go into full detail here on how to hunt and forage with the primitive tools and weapons you make. However, if you have no notion of how to actually hunt with the spear, bow, or throwing stick you've made, those tools will do you little good. The following brief instructions, if diligently applied, will aid you in becoming a successful survival-level hunter/forager, and to better sense, experience, and enjoy your immediate environment.

* A version of these instructions and another short story illustrating how to hunt in this way appears in another one of my books, *An Introduction to Firearms*, in the chapter, *The Tao of Hunting*. In that story I describe how I took a mule deer with a handgun in an area that had been abandoned by other hunters as "having no game."

To hunt successfully with the weapons our distant ancestors used, you must hunt as they did, and as some aboriginal people still do today—by being tuned into, and being part of, their environment. This allows them, and will allow you, to see, hear, smell, and sense everything around them and to move through their area without alarming every animal within ten miles.

The average urbanite, suburbanite, or even country person tramps through field and forest like a trumpeting elephant, taking no care

to move quietly, no notice of the wind or the details and texture of the immediate environment, and having no awareness of the wild creatures around them. The same applies to many village people in less developed nations who have lost touch with the natural world.

Most hikers and backpackers, many of whom think of themselves as experienced outdoors persons, stay to established trails and stomp along talking loudly, sometimes even playing music, and treating the wilderness as a diorama, something to be observed rather than interacted with. Although backpackers might spend a good deal of time passing through wilderness areas, rarely do they have much awareness of the world around them. As a consequence, they miss seeing most wild creatures and most of the wonder that surrounds them. Some even wear bear bells designed to alert bears of their presence and in theory frighten them away. I don't know how well that strategy works with bears. Given that backpackers are instructed to give their packs to bears if approached, I suspect those bells sound like dinner bells to bears. Certainly those bells succeed in alerting every other creature within hearing, most of which will either run away, hide, or freeze in place and observe these odd musical creatures.

Awareness

To develop awareness in wild places, when entering any new area, whether hunting or in a survival situation or just out for the day, take time to tune into your environment. Stand or sit quietly for a few minutes and extend your **perception** as far as you can, across meadows, through woods, up the mountainside. See in your mind's eye what you cannot see with your vision, and feel the vibe of the area.

See the movement of treetop leaves in the wind, and watch for animal sign: tracks, droppings, cracked nut shells on the ground and the squirrel's nest in the tree above, a patch bare of bark on a tree where a deer has rubbed his antlers, the small path through weeds that leads to a rabbit den.

Hear the chipmunk skittering through dry leaves, the splash of a fish in a nearby pond, the grunting of wild boar, the breathing of the fox that's watching you, the drip of early morning dew from the limbs above you.

Clear your nose, flare your nostrils, and **smell** the cold granite or musty leaves, or the tannin from the dark swampy stream behind you, the rank odor of a bear, the sweet scent of ripe berries, the dry musk of a snake.

Feel the wind on your face, and the caress of green needles on your arm as you move past a pine tree, the smooth bark of a birch tree under your fingertips, the dry crumbling edge of an old raccoon track.

Think about where the animal that left their sign might be, and how you can approach it, or avoid it if it might be dangerous.

Moving and Being

As important as activating your sensorium, you must become part of your environment. Move *with* the wind and the forest. Move as a cat moves, smoothly, your entire body integrated and flowing. Step softly and lightly, feeling the ground underfoot. Do not city walk; you're not on a sidewalk. Do not slam your heels into the earth or stand tall and stride like the lord of all creation. Move in the shadow of boulders or with trees to break the outline of your silhouette.

▲ Try to observe the world around you. Credit: Steven Pavlov, CC BY-SA 4.0.

Do not think of yourself as an intruder, a lost city person, or someone on the edge of panic and desperately striving to survive. This vibe will radiate from you and every creature within range will pick up on it and move away from you, or freeze in place until you're gone. Think of yourself as being a natural part of everything around you, as being at home wherever you are, and then *be* at home. Be fully engaged, aware, and present in the moment. Animals may well sense your presence, but it won't be as alarming to them as it would be if you were stomping and crashing through their neighborhood radiating panic or desperation.

The animals that rely on their sense of smell will smell you. But you can mitigate their awareness of your foreignness by rubbing your clothing with whatever aromatic plants grow in the area: pine needles, oak or willow leaves, and so on. Doing this will help to make you blend into and become part of the area. Don't be shy if you happen on a patch of wild lavender. Rub it into your clothing and carry some in your pockets, and it will go a long way toward screening your human scent. It will also help repel bugs. Just make sure you're not using poison ivy or some other poisonous plant. Also, keep as clean as you can to reduce your scent. Wash in cold water if that's all you have available.

If you are actively hunting, rather than being alert for targets of opportunity as you travel, move toward your quarry with the wind in your face if at all possible. In a survival situation, hunt by keeping all your senses activated, moving smoothly and quietly, and watching for opportunity while moving towards your destination. Such opportunity hunting, and foraging, often pays great dividends.

If remaining at one location while awaiting help, and if you're not injured in a way that prevents movement, picking a likely location where there is animal sign and waiting for game to pass by might be your best strategy. This is most workable at first light before moving out, and at last light before settling in for the night. In this instance you must remain alert while you sit, lie, or stand without moving. If you haven't practiced the art of stillness, you might think you're not moving when you probably are. A deer can spot the flicker of an eyelid at fifty yards. When you first try to be still, direct your attention to each part of your body, especially your fingers, toes, and head. If you keep those extremities still, your arms, legs, and body will most likely also be still. Blink your eyes slowly. Breath slowly and deeply.

Select a spot where you can blend into the background. Attaching a few branches to your clothing and leaves to your hat and clothing so they break up your outline can be quite helpful. Wherever you are, mentally blend into the background. If your back is to a tree, imagine yourself sinking into the trunk and becoming part of the tree. Put your roots deep into the earth, feel your branches spreading, and think long, slow green thoughts. If you're concealed among rocks, imagine yourself as one of them, a solid unmoving rock that has lain in place for thousands of years as all the living things of the world passed by. This kind of thinking reduces your human vibe, and by subsuming your consciousness into a tree or rock, reduces the predator energy hunters radiate.

Employ these methods and you will have a good chance of getting close to wild animals. Then, like a cat, you must pounce when you get close. Watch how cats, those highly successful sight hunters, locate prey, stalk, and take it. Move slowly when drawing back your spear for a thrust, or your stick for a throw. Then thrust or throw quickly, smoothly, and with power. If you haven't been spotted, pull your bowstring slowly and release smoothly.

I've used these methods since I was a child. I stumbled upon them when I was trying to emulate the way I imagined Indians would hunt, and by watching cats. By the time I was twelve I had taken a good deal of small game (there was no large game near the farming communities where I grew up) by using this approach—and with primitive weapons, more in fact than my friends who hunted in groups with rifles and shotguns. I had also come to know the woods and the lives of the creatures that lived there and to sense the flow of life in nature and to feel myself being a part of that flow.

Life and Death

Everything alive fights for its life. If you take on the task and responsibility of killing an animal close up with a spear or stick, you will have to confront and deal with the animal's struggle for its life, its cries, its pain. It will not be like the sanitized deaths of hunted animals you may have seen on screen. There will be blood. It will not be pretty.

Boys did not cry when I grew up in the Midwest and South. It just wasn't done. Boys' roles were well defined. Boys were expected to hunt, play ball, have fist fights, and do boy stuff. Getting bruises and broken bones was just part of being a boy. Crying was not. I cried when I killed my first wild creature. I heard its cries and felt its pain and fear as its life leaked away. I was alone and glad to be alone and ashamed of my tears. I never wanted to kill anything again. But I knew I had to toughen up to get through life. I did. But I have never taken any creature's

life without feeling its pain. I console myself with the understanding that all life must take other life to live (even plants kill to live) and that I am not above or apart from that process but a part of it, no more or less important than the plankton in the sea or the earthworms under my feet. That's the flow of our universe, and part of the Tao. Be aware when you take life of what you are doing. If you've never hunted or killed an animal, be prepared. You might have an emotional reaction.

A Story of the Tao of the Hunt

I was first exposed to Chinese martial arts and Taoist philosophy and practices when I was fifteen through a high school friend who introduced me to his uncle, who was a martial arts master from Canton Province in China. I learned that what I had been doing in the woods amounted to unschooled sitting and moving meditation. When my friend's uncle accepted me as a student, I began to train in formal methods of meditation, awareness, and focus, in addition to Kung Fu, and to practice on my own. I have continued this training with various teachers, and in solitary practice, all of my life. From the beginning I incorporated these formal teachings into my youthful methods of hunting and awareness. Over time these practices influenced every part of my life and became part of my being. The skills so acquired served me well in military service and afterwards, and saved my life more than once. These skills also intensified my perception of our world and helped to enable me to take great joy in perceiving its wonder and magic.

During the sixties I spent a quite bit of time in Mexico with a good friend, Raphael, who was from Mexico City. With the blessings of Raphael's uncle, who was a director of the national anthropology museum, we set off on a more or less amateur expedition in the Yucatan to locate a long-abandoned Mayan city.

There were just the two of us and two Lacandon Indians, Ikal and Kabi, who we recruited as guides in Merida, the capitol city of Yucatan, and Antonio, whom we also recruited in Merida. Antonio was of Mayan decent, had grown up in Merida, and spoke Mayan and Spanish. The Lacandons spoke no Spanish. Neither Raphael nor I spoke any Mayan.

The Lacandon are one of the Mayan groups, and at that time not much studied by anthropologists, as they since have been. At that time most Lacandons lived in villages, practiced slash-and-burn agriculture and subsistence hunting, and lived in deep poverty. As part of their religion, they drank home-brewed alcohol and tranced out on mushrooms containing psilocybin, a hallucinogenic. They also sacrificed animals to their gods. Rumor had it that they still practiced human sacrifice and cannibalism deep in jungle hideaways.

Ikal and Kabi, like other Lacandons we met, were quite small, about five feet tall and thin, with long, straight black hair hanging to their shoulders. Both had deep-set dark eyes that slid away from mine. Antonio told us that the Lacandon didn't like to look directly into another person's eyes. They considered it rude. They wore sandals and long caftan-like garments made with hand-woven cotton. Ikal had a bow and arrows he had made. He was missing two fingers from his left hand. Kabi had a deep scar running down his calf. His right foot had been broken and was twisted. Both had numerous small scars that told of hard lives. They smelled of old sweat and woodsmoke.

Ikal told us, through Antonio, that he was the most successful hunter of his village and would supplement our food supply while in the bush. At the market we purchased corn meal, tortillas, jerky, avocados, dried beans, squash, and some fruit, which our local guides assured us would be adequate for the journey. Ikal and Kabi each had a gourd filled with home-brewed alcohol suffused with, they said through Antonio as best as we could understand, the "child spirit." By which they meant psilocybin mushrooms.

We also bought string hammocks, mosquito nets, lightweight tarps to hang over the hammocks, dried gourds for use as canteens, machetes for each of us, a cook pot, and a few odds and ends. Part of the price that we agreed upon for Ikal's and Kabi's services was a machete for each of them, which we gave to them before departure, and all of the other equipment when we returned. Raphael was uneasy about the machetes. He said these people hated the Spanish, and with good reason given their history of exploitation by Spanish conquerors, and that they might kill us in our sleep. Antonio said that the Lacandons were violent among themselves but he did not think they would cause us any problems. Raphael and I were both armed. We agreed to take turns keeping watch and decided to go ahead.

Raphael's uncle had given us an unreliable map to the site we sought. Based on estimates by Antonio, and by Ikal and Kabi, neither of whom could read a map, it appeared we could reach the site in two to three days on foot. We planned to be on site for about the same length of time, and then return. All in all, the trip should take about six to nine days.

We eventually did find the site, after six days of thrashing through the bush and being feasted upon by every insect in the Yucatan. The area we were in was mostly scrub, rather than classic triple-canopy jungle, and was home to many birds and small animals, plus a thriving population of many, many forms of insects, all of which seemed to prefer us to other types of nourishment. I have no idea what these bugs ate before we arrived.

The Lacandons, being so small, moved through the brush with relative ease, but made as much noise as any city person and appeared to have little idea of where we were or where we were going. I used my compass and kept a route map and was able to determine that we had almost boxed the compass (traveled north, south, east, and west) by the time we found the site. I had watched the Lacandons closely, even from my hammock after the fire died. Neither showed any signs of ill intent.

The day we found the site we were down to about a kilo of cornmeal and a small bag of dried beans. The jerky and the rest of our provisions had all been consumed. Ikal had gone off into the forest each morning before we set out, but brought in no game. Given that he appeared to be half tranced most of the time, this did not surprise me. Each night Ikal and Kabi drank from their gourds around the fire and went to sleep, or passed out, after eating.

I had previously lived for some weeks and hunted with the Huichol Indians in Nayarit in northern Mexico. They call themselves the "deer people." The men consume peyote cactus in the belief it brings them closer to the spirit of the deer. That might be so, but when I

was with them we ate tortillas and beans. No venison. Their kids were noticeably undernourished. Some showed signs of rickets. A group of anthropologists from the US were studying the Huichol at the same time I was there. The professors were reverent and respectful regarding the Huichol religion and much impressed by their "oneness with nature and the deer." None of the professors lived or hunted with the Huichol, and they all ate at their hotel, not with the Indians. I had not been impressed with the notion that hallucinogens could do much of anything to help feed the Huichol kids or in any way ensure success in the physical world, or even to be "one with nature." In the same way, the "spirit of the mushroom" seemed to do nothing to help the Lacandon to cope with the world they lived in. Both the Huichol men and Lacandon men appeared to be lost in their own minds and about as generally competent as the average skid-row drunk.

Raphael and I were excited about finding the site, not a grand city, but nevertheless an actual Mayan pyramid long overgrown with vines and shrubbery. The Lacandons were bored; they had seen all this. They did help with their machetes and cleared enough overgrowth to allow photos, however. In addition to being excited about the find, we were hungry. Not starving, but very hungry. Antonio nagged at Ikal, the designated hunter, to go out and get us some food, anything.

Ikal departed our camp that first evening after locating the site in search of game. He returned shortly after dark, empty-handed and nervous. The Lacandons greatly feared the jaguars that prowled this country, and the spirits of the night. They stayed close to the fire after dark. As usual, he and Kabi drank from their gourds and went to sleep, or into a trance. It was hard to tell the difference.

The next morning Antonio roused Ikal and sent him out again to hunt. He returned from his hunt with a brightly colored bird, which was plucked and stewed. It provided little nourishment for five hungry men, and it did not taste like chicken. During six days of hiking and two days on site, even though Ikal went hunting each day, this was his entire take: a parrot.

If Ikal was the best hunter in his village, I could imagine what their diet must have been. No wonder they were so small and thin and looked undernourished. Neither Lacandon had exhibited much situational awareness, or in any way showed they had much understanding of their environment. As far as I could tell, they had taken little or no note of the noises in the bush that clearly were made by animals of various kinds. In addition to the noise the animals made, I could *feel* animal life all around us. Anyone the least bit tuned into the world around us could. Neither commented or took note of the game trails, animal tracks, and droppings we had passed. They were village people, not forest Indians. The fact that they got stoned each night and seemed to be more or less tranced during the day did not aid them in environmental awareness. In addition to the many indications I had seen of forest life, a local hunter with a single-shot .22 rifle and a small deer over his shoulder had boarded

▲ A jaguar in South America. Credit: Charles J. Sharp, CC BY-SA 4.0.

our bus when we were leaving Merida. I *knew* there were animals in the bush.

Raphael was a city guy, raised in Mexico City, educated at the Sorbonne and UCLA. He had been uneasy and uncomfortable during the entire time we had been in the bush. Antonio was also a city guy. If we were going to get any more food before our return to Merida, it was up to me. Everyone wanted me to try my luck.

I went into instructor mode and through Antonio tried to interest Ikal in awakening his senses and going hunting with me. I thought doing so would help him to become a better hunter and better take care of his family. He just looked through me. It appeared to me that he had spent so much time pursuing mushroom dreams in his mind that he couldn't connect with the physical world. Kabi made a comment that, translated, said, "You can easy kill anything with your *pistola.*" The gulf between the Spanish, and gringos by extension, and the Indians, was wide and deep. The Indians attributed much of the power of the Spanish to their firearms. *Pistolas* seemed to be regarded as magic wands.

It was then that I decided to hunt with Ikal's bow. It was a poor weapon. A spear would be about as efficient. I thought that if I could show him that even I, a gringo, could be successful with his gear, he might wake up and take an interest. Then we might even make some improvements to his equipment. Ikal readily gave me his bow but declined to accompany me.

I went to a spring a couple of hundred meters west of the site where I had seen animal tracks. The water was cool in the shade of low scrub trees and carried a green scent, like the thick vegetation hanging over most of it. There were many animal tracks around the edge.

Wild pigs had churned the bank into mud. There were little handprints, tracks made by either a raccoon or coatimundi, and fox or dog tracks, I couldn't tell the difference, and what I was hoping for—deer tracks. Sharp edged, they were recent tracks of the small Yucatan deer. I had also hoped for jaguar tracks. Not that I wanted to kill or eat one, but because I had had a recent encounter with a jaguar, a caged one I had set free. And because a Zapotec shaman had told me that jaguars would not harm me, that the jaguar was my *tonal,* soul ally. I didn't know whether to believe the shaman or not but I intensely wanted to encounter a jaguar in the wild.

Circling the spring, I found a clear, well-used game trail. I moved slowly along the trail, covering maybe one hundred meters an hour, following a thin line of deer tracks. The footing was soft, and I moved quietly, my eyes scanning for tracks, droppings, movement, shape. My ears were attuned for a footfall, for the sound of movement in the brush. All my senses were fully engaged. The air was still, thick, heavy, humid, no hint of a breeze. Gnats swarmed around my head. Sweat poured over my body. "Wait a minute vines" and thorns pulled at my clothing. After a couple of hours, I came to a thick stand of saplings and underbrush where the game trail faded into an intersection of smaller trails and wandering tracks. There were fresh droppings where the trail ended. I stopped, and continued to look, listen, and feel. I sensed nothing but small birds in the immediate area, but felt that there might be something deeper in the brush or on the other side of the stand.

Going to my knees, I crawled slowly into the brush. Thick vines impeded my forward motion and I carefully moved them aside. I avoided the spider webs as best I could, and with great care moved through those I couldn't. There were spiders scampering every which way. None of them bit me so I didn't die. All spiders are poisonous. You knew that, right? Spiders are not my friends. My senses were also alert for snakes. Rattlesnakes, coral snakes, hog-nosed vipers, and other poisonous snakes are endemic to the Yucatan and feared by locals. Feared by me too.

I went to my belly, and with Ikal's bow and three arrows in my left hand, low crawled deeper and deeper into the stand of brush. Stopping frequently to keep my breathing slow and quiet, I directed most of my attention and perception to the far side of the stand, while keeping awareness expanded all around me. I continued, now moving at an earthworm's speed. Dirt collected in the sweat of my body and got under my belt and rubbed along my belly. I could smell the fresh green scent of the weeds being crushed under me and hear the faint scrape of the weeds on my clothing, as well as the scritching of tiny birds as they hopped from limb to limb above me and the hum of mosquitos as they vectored in on me. Hummingbird-sized mosquitos disturbed from their midday nests swarmed around me and sucked blood from my face, neck, and hands. Ants crawled over me and into my clothing. A cricket-like bug five times as big as any cricket took a bite of my hand. I slowly crushed it. Vengeance is sweet. As I rested for a minute or so, I heard movement deeper in the brush.

I relaxed into the earth on my stomach, closed my eyes, breathed deeply and slowly, and let my mind drift outwards. I could *feel* something alive about ten meters ahead of me. I slithered forward on my belly. It probably took a half hour to cover the next few meters. Keeping my eyes soft, my attention wide and soft, trying to not project a predator's vibe, I finally reached a spot where I could see through a gap in the brush and into a small clearing. Three deer were resting in their beds, the closest one about five meters from me. Moving at glacial speed, I came up into a kneeling position, keeping a screen of brush between me and the clearing. Moving carefully and slower than slow, I drew an arrow, focused on a spot on the chest of the closest deer and released it through a tiny opening in the brush. The arrow struck and penetrated a few inches above my focus spot.

The deer jumped to his feet, faltered, and fell. The other deer—two more were revealed when they jumped to their feet from the concealing brush—disappeared in a flash, crashing through the undergrowth. I ran to the downed deer and finished the kill with my machete. I got some bruises from his hooves as he fought his last fight. One raised a lump the size of a tennis ball on my forehead. Fair enough. Sorry, my friend, it was your time. He was a buck, about the size of a large German shepherd, average size for the Yucatan. I quickly field dressed him and carried him back to camp.

I had hunted with Ikal's bow rather than my handgun to show him and Kabi that it wasn't possession of a magic weapon that insured success, and that if he roused himself from his trance he could be a better provider for his family. In the end it was apparent that my efforts meant nothing to him and came to nothing, other than a meal of fresh venison and a few pounds of jerky dried over a low fire to see us back to Merida. My route map made it obvious we had been wandering all over the area and were not far from our starting point. I plotted a more direct return and two days of walking brought us to the road where we had dropped off the bus outside of Merida.

Many years later I became friends with a well-known experimental archeologist who told me that the Lacandon were a degenerate culture, and that due to their practice of consuming quantities of psilocybin had become so lost in their interior world that they were barely able to function in the physical world.

The point to this story is that awareness, attention, focus, and intention are more important to survival hunting success, or indeed survival, than tools. I described the scent of water, the thorns, the spiders, sweat, and heat, the sound of weeds being crushed, to show how you should be aware of everything around you. Ikal's bow didn't amount to much, a simple sapling with about a thirty-pound pull. The arrows were cane with hardwood foreshafts, tipped with knapped stone and fletched with parrot feathers. Anyone with a decent blade and minimal skill could make such a bow and a few arrows in a morning's work. I am a mediocre archer at best. I was able to get to meat where a local person with local knowledge was unsuccessful, and using his poor equipment, by utilizing skills that are primarily mental. Anyone who practices the skills I advocate could have similar success at survival-level hunting, and at surviving anyplace in the physical world.

Opportunistic Hunting and Foraging

Sport hunters seek a specific game animal—deer, elk, pheasant, rabbit, or whatever—and must conform to hunting regulations regarding when and where they can legally hunt. A survival hunter/forager makes no such distinction and seeks anything he can eat or use—lizards, snakes, small and large animals, nuts and berries, raw materials to improve his situation—and is alert to opportunity at all times.

An accompanying photo in the section on containers (see page 105) shows a few things I gathered during an hour's walk in a Bulgarian forest in the foothills of the Stara Planina Mountains while scouting for wild boar sign: rose hips, which can be eaten fresh or cooked, or used for a tea; acorns, which can be eaten after leaching out the tannin by soaking; walnuts and hazelnuts, which only have to be opened to eat; an old rakia bottle, which I could use for a water bottle or improvised knife or arrowheads; a scrap of newspaper for tinder; clumps of sheep wool, enough to make a belly band to warm the *tan tien* (a spot just below and behind your navel that is the center of balance and heat generation), and donkey hair for a bowstring. While foraging all of these useful things, I also spotted a squirrel's nest, a large hare, and wild boar tracks. I followed the boar tracks to a deep canyon where a herd was resting. I left them in peace and they never knew I was there.

Another photo shows a stand of Nopal cactus I happened upon while stalking a desert sheep for a photo. I was in the Mojave, where desert sheep are protected—photos yes, hunting no, unless in a survival situation. This cactus is quite useful. The pads can be cooked or eaten raw as salad, and the fruit is quite tasty raw. Just be careful when removing the needles. A knife with a longer blade would be useful for this task, as would a couple of whittled sticks used like chopsticks to handle the pads until you remove the needles. This single plant contains

▲ Buck Compadre cutting spines off of a nopal cactus pad.

enough calories to feed two people for many days.

Lizards like the one in the photo scampered over rocks near the cactus. It would have been a simple matter to collect a dozen lizards with a few whacks of a throwing stick or jabs with a spear. Cooked over an open fire, those lizards, along with nopal pads, would be enough for dinner for two, saving the fruit for dessert. If I had been hunting the sheep for food, and

▲ Possible lunch?

missed him, we could still have fed ourselves on the cactus and lizards. This is a primary difference between the survival hunter and the sport hunter, who would have counted the day as lost if he missed the sheep.

There was a water seep nearby and ample shade. If we had been awaiting rescue, we could have stayed there and survived quite well by collecting lizards and cooking them with cactus for at least a week, probably longer. There was plenty of other wildlife in the area, as was evident by the many tracks that small mammals and birds made when they came each evening to the water seep. Those too could be taken by spear and throwing stick.

These brief instructions and my story about hunting in the Yucatan should put you in the right frame of mind to shift into aboriginal hunter/forager mode. Civilization as we know it is only about 12,000 years old. Humans were hunters and gatherers for at least half a million years before that. An aboriginal hunter/forager lies buried deep within most of us.

There's more, a lot more. I can identify the particular edible plants I mentioned without any doubt. I know how to safely process lizards for eating. If you want to learn more about these topics, start by reading the books in Suggested Reading at the back of this book. If you want deeper knowledge, seek hands-on instruction from the sources recommended in those books. If you want to learn how to activate all of your senses, how to blend with your environment, to move silently and sense everything in your immediate area, read my book, *The Tao of Survival*, and do the lessons in it.

Notes

- Ninety percent of all wild plants are inedible. Many are poisonous. Many that are poisonous resemble edible plants so closely that only an expert can distinguish them. Do not eat any wild plant you cannot positively identify.
- It's best to cook all wild plants, except berries and nuts. For example, snails lay their eggs on watercress. If cooked, those eggs are a bit of protein. If not, they can become internal parasites.
- Almost all wild animals are edible.
- Do not eat salamanders, as most are poisonous, or toads, many of which are toxic.
- All reptiles carry salmonella on their skin, and must be processed with care. Hands must be thoroughly washed after handling them. Failure to do so can result in severe illness.
- Most insects are edible, but most of them carry parasites. To be safe, eat no insect without cooking it. Remove chitinous parts.
- Virtually all creatures need water. Quietly following a steam or river, or hiding near a pond, will often enable you to locate animals. Predators often lie in wait near water to ambush the herbivores that must

come to water. You can do the same. If no mammals are about, fish, crustaceans, and amphibians can be taken and eaten.
- After handling any food, wash your hands. Failing to do so will draw insects.
- A trick I learned many years ago from an old World War II jungle fighter who later taught survival, is to only touch meat or game with one hand, keeping the other hand, your knife hand, clean. Keeping one hand clean helps to ensure that you do not touch any of your gear with the hand that handled meat. Doing so will draw insects. If you allow a residue from meat, or any food, to get on your clothing or gear you will likely find yourself covered in bugs. Also, you DO NOT want to smell of meat, fish, or any food, in bear or big cat country.

Traps and Snares

Since this is a book on survival knives and their use, we cannot detail the dozens of different kinds of traps used all over the world. Detailed instructions on many traps and snares can be found in the Suggested Reading at the back of this book.

Whereas hunting and fishing are active methods of taking game (and can be done while on the move), trapping and snaring are passive in that the trap can operate without your presence and without your having to take any further action after setting the trap. Successful trapping requires a good bit of local knowledge about animals and their habits, the ability to craft good traps, and the skill to set them where they'll produce. You can acquire local knowledge by the methods detailed in the section on tuning in and blending with your environment, by careful observation, from local people, and by research in advance of need.

Snares, which are nooses set in a location where animals travel, require very tough cordage, or a length of that wire or dental floss you have in your pocket. There are dozens of different ways to rig a snare. A word of caution: The twitch-up snare often put forth as the most effective all-around trap is dependent upon a trail where game passes, a sapling close at hand, cordage, a perfectly sized noose for the animal to be taken, and a good snap to break the animals neck. I do not recommend this snare for the survivor. It requires too many variables to be effective in a variety of different environments. Snares that do not kill the animal at once will enable it to chew the cordage and free itself, unless you're using wire, or are on the spot to take them at once. Setting many snares in a small area where you've determined that game is present, and then driving them into the snares, can be effective.

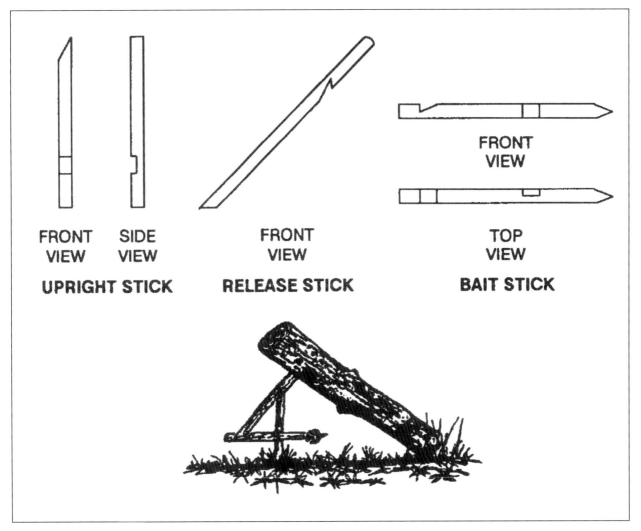

FRONT VIEW   SIDE VIEW

UPRIGHT STICK

FRONT VIEW

RELEASE STICK

FRONT VIEW

TOP VIEW

BAIT STICK

▲ Figure-four deadfall.

Everybody and his cousin has seen the figure-four deadfall in survival books, on television survival shows, and in every Boy Scout, Girl Scout, or other outdoor program that exists. Over the years I have found the figure-four to be the easiest trap for students to make and remember, and the one that produces the most reliable results in a wide variety of environments. The figure-four can be rigged anyplace there are scraps of wood and heavy objects, and it can be baited so that the animal will come to the trap. Thus it is location dependent only in that it must be set in an area where there is game.

That said, traps are not the survivor's best chance of getting food unless he's stuck in one location. Setting traps each night while on the move is not workable. Further, making a trap of any kind without a knife to cut wood, carve triggers and notches is pretty much a nonstarter. There are experts in primitive survival who can first knap out a stone blade (requiring more time and calories) and make traps with that blade. That's probably not you, unless you've had training and much practice. Have a knife. Even if you're not going to make traps, have a knife.

Urban and Fringe Area Usage

When most people think of needing a survival knife, they're thinking of wilderness use, which is understandable given that each year hundreds of people get lost or otherwise find themselves in life-threatening situations in the wilderness—and that's just in the US. Travelers, and local people who live near wilderness in Latin America, Africa, and parts of Asia, also frequently get into wilderness survival situations. But in today's mobile and fast-moving world, anyone can find him or herself in a survival situation at any time and any place. Six of the eight instances cited in the introduction to this book took place in urban or fringe areas. I personally know of many more occurrences when a knife enabled a person to survive a life-threatening event in areas that were not wilderness, than those that took place in the wilderness.

Chapter Nine

Self-Defense from People and Animals with the Blade

*T*he United States is a gun culture, rather than a blade culture. Many countries in the East and in Asia are blade cultures and hold the blade in higher esteem as a weapon of defense and aggression. There is an old saying in the East, "The gun is your friend. The knife is your brother." The meaning is apparent. A gun can run out of ammunition, is more complicated, and is less dependable. The knife can be always relied upon and should be held close. There's also an old saying in the States: "Don't bring a knife to a gunfight." That saying assumes you will have access to a gun, which you might well have—in the US. This is not always so in other countries, where firearms are tightly controlled and not available to the general population. Both sayings are reflective of their cultures.

In truth the blade is a formidable weapon whether used in defense or offense. Police guidelines in many US jurisdictions state that an attacker with a knife who's within twenty-one feet should be considered a lethal threat. However, this does not mean that if you're confronted by a criminal with a gun you should try to overwhelm him with your survival knife.

I do not advocate for anyone to use a blade in defense. A blade is considered lethal force almost everywhere. Even in South America, Mexico, and Spain, which are to a certain extent blade cultures, and where the knife is classed as an *arma blanca*, a white arm, rather than an *arma del fuego*, a firearm, the deployment of a blade is considered potential lethal force. In fact, using a blade in a violent encounter with man or beast can lead to death. And so, the decision to do so is a grave one, and must be made by the individual according to circumstances and conscience.

The subject of self-defense with a blade is large, complicated, and beyond the limits of this book. There are shelves of books devoted to this subject. For an introduction to the topic, and to learn a simple, effective method of self-defense with a blade, one that I've taught *pro bono* to rape survivors referred to me by a rape crisis center, and to noncombatants who must go in harm's way, I refer you to one of my other books, *The Tactical Knife* (Skyhorse Publishing, 2014). I've trained in blade arts, but my qualifications for teaching these skills come from real-world experience in which I've been obliged to defend my life with a blade.

I have taught this method in one-day seminars, and some of my students later used it to defend their persons and/or lives. This simple, easy-to-learn approach to self-defense with the blade is not any type of martial art or fencing. Rather, it uses natural reflexive movements that the body instinctively reverts to when attacked, and enables small or weaker persons to overcome and escape larger, stronger attackers, and multiple attackers.

If you have a need or desire to learn self-defense with the blade beyond this basic method, there are a few qualified instructors who teach it. They can be found on the Internet. A word of caution if you're seeking training in self-defense *from* an attack with a blade: Many martial arts instructors teach blade-disarming methods that at best do not work and at worst will get you killed. The simplest way to determine if a given defensive technique is effective, or to determine the effectiveness of any technique, is to do it at full speed with a training blade—against resistance. Truth will be revealed.

For our purposes, take it as given that any blade, even a small one, can be a fearsomely effective defensive weapon. I once knew a twelve-year-old boy who was taken by a sexual predator whose stated intentions were to rape and kill him. While his would-be rapist and murderer was distracted and fighting to take off the boy's clothing, he managed to get out his pocketknife, an ordinary little folder, and severely wound this monster. While his assailant was screaming and bleeding, the boy unlocked the door and ran, barely escaping with his life. This frightened child had no training to guide him, just fear, anger, and determination to save himself, qualities anyone can draw upon. If so threatened, take heart and overcome.

I mentioned the danger of feral dog packs in a previous section of this book. I've not seen effective defensive tactics for this situation available anywhere else in print. And so, since this information might save your life, here is some possibly critical information on the

▲ You never know if wild dog packs are friendly or aggressive, so you should be prepared. Credit: Ivan Bandura, CC BY 2.0.

subject, information that I have gained through experience. Feral dog packs, part jackal or otherwise, are a danger in the Balkans, most of Eastern Europe, Russia, India, Southeast Asia, and other parts of the world, in rural areas and in cities. As an example, Sofia, the capitol city of Bulgaria, is estimated to have over ten thousand stray dogs, some which form packs and attack people. Feral dog packs killed three people during the last couple of years in Sofia. In 2017, a British woman was attacked, killed, and partially eaten by a pack of feral dogs at a tourist site near Athens, Greece. I visited Greece that same year and saw aggressive packs of feral dogs roaming the streets near the Acropolis. The cops I talked to about the attack on the British woman just shrugged their shoulders. The situation is worse in rural Asia and the Middle East.

Many "experts" advise that you should avoid eye contact and be submissive if attacked by a dog or dogs, the notion being that the dog or dogs will then leave you alone. This is bad advice—in fact dangerous advice. A pack of dogs that is attacking you, or about to attack, are not nice doggies just barking to defend their suburban yards. They have gone feral and will injure or kill you if they can. If they bring you down and kill you, and if no one stops them, they will eat you. Think of them as canine psychopathic cannibals. Being submissive in the face of a dog attack can get you severely mauled, or killed, especially if attacked by a pack. You must dominate the dog, or dogs, and be prepared to fight if necessary. I've been attacked by packs of feral dogs on a number of occasions and as a result have developed defensive tactics for this threat.

Some points:

- Dogs that grab a person's arm, as you might have seen in videos, have been trained to do so. Feral dogs, like jackals, and like wolves, do not attack in this way.
- Dog, jackal, and wolf packs circle and look for weak spots and try to attack from behind.
- They will first attack in low line, that is, below the waist. If they can pull you down, they will then go for your torso, throat, and face.
- The alpha, the dominant dog in the pack, will lead the initial attack, and then often will circle while the other pack members try to bring you down. If they accomplish that, the alpha will rush in to kill.

Defensive tactics if you have only your survival knife:

- If attacked, accept that you will have to fight. Commit to doing so with full aggression. Do not turn your back and run. You cannot outrun a dog or a pack of dogs.
- If attacked, deploy your knife at once. Keep your blade between yourself and the threat. Do NOT attempt to use the so-called reverse grip with the blade extending from the lower part of your hand like an icepick. Hold your knife like a sword. Use controlled slashes as you advance, attack, and retreat to back cover. Use thrusts only on defense when one of the animals is coming at you and is within striking range.
- If possible, get your back to a wall, tree, boulder, auto, or anything that offers cover from rear attack. If you cannot get cover for your back, stay light on your feet, be

prepared to quickly turn in a circle. While doing so, keep awareness all around you. Beware of pack members circling to your back.

- Attack the alpha if he's within reach. If you can wound, kill, or otherwise chase off the alpha, the others will follow. If you cannot reach the alpha, attack the dog closest to you.

- If there are stones or other projectiles available, and if you can reach them without going low and exposing yourself further, use them. Throw with force with the hand not using your knife to hit and injure the alpha.

- Do not attempt to "give a dog your weak arm," as "experts" advise. They are unlikely to go for your arm, but if they do the resulting pain and injury can be incapacitating. Moreover, while you're dealing with the one dog, or jackal, or wolf, that has your arm and is trying to bring you down, the others will be circling and attacking in low line from all directions.

- If you have martial arts training, fight from a strong, low horse. If not, fight from a deep crouch. Do NOT bend from the waist, as doing so brings your throat and face closer to their teeth.

- Draw blood from the alpha and the fight might be over. It also might not be, depending on how aggressive the alpha is.

- Do not tunnel vision and focus only on the dog with which you are immediately engaged to the exclusion of the pack. Keep a wide perspective and use your peripheral vision to keep track of all pack members.

- While keeping your back to cover, if any, keep moving. Avoid being a static target.

- A pack can, and sometimes does, circle and continue to attack for an extended period and follow if you're moving away from them. You may need to call on your reserves of endurance. Your best chance is to damage the alpha.

- Yell at the dogs and call for help while fighting, but do not count on help arriving. Accept that you might have to overcome this attack on your own. Do not give up.

- Obviously a long-bladed knife is better than one with a short blade for this type of encounter. Many dogs, jackals, and wolves have muzzles longer than a four-inch bladed utility knife. Even if you strike them in the mouth, their fangs can still reach, lacerate, and possibly immobilize your knife hand. However, any blade astronomically improves your odds of surviving and overcoming in this kind of fight.

The above assumes you do not have a staff or spear. If you have either, adjust your tactics accordingly. Come to think about it, these are good tactics if attacked by a pack of feral humans.

Defense with a knife from other wild animals, such as mountain lions or bears, should be considered a desperate last-chance attempt to survive. That said, there are many true accounts of people killing large, wild animals, including mountain lions and bears, with knives. Wild boar are often hunted and killed with large blades. There's even one famous instance of a man killing an African lion with his six-inch bladed hunting knife while being mauled, and surviving. If attacked by any animal, and if armed with only a knife, even a folder, go all in and give it your best. Ignore

▲ Know whether your knife is legal for travel before you get to security, especially in American airports like this one.

wounds and fight. Humans are not prey unless we allow ourselves to be. Fight for your life. In doing so, you might retain it.

Legalities: Knives, Laws, and Travel

Since I write about travel, and about knives, I receive many emails from readers asking if they can take their knives with them to Europe or South America or Southeast Asia. I understand. You always have a knife handy. It's your basic tool. Without it, how do you open packages, or cut anything? How can you get through your day without a knife? What if you need your knife to punch out the window of an overturned bus, or escape from a burning building? What about that picnic next to the Canal du Midi, or on the train. You don't want to be reduced to ripping and tearing at salami, cheese, and baguettes with teeth and nails. You need your knife. But, you don't know the laws and regulations in Europe or in other countries,

and you're a law-abiding person. So, can you take your knife with you? Yes, you can. But, there are some things you need to know.

In the United States, laws and regulations concerning knives are a confusing patchwork that varies from state to state, county to county, town to town, and which make no sense whatsoever. It is not possible to travel from California to New York with any kind of knife without violating a law or regulation in some place along the way. Few of those laws and regulations are actually enforced. Enforcement is determined by decisions made by the individual police officer. Those decisions will vary from officer to officer, according to his perception of you and the situation. It's about the same in Europe, although it can be somewhat different in the rest of the world.

Since most Americans who travel internationally travel to Europe, I'll first comment on European laws and customs, and then on other countries and regions with which I'm familiar. The European Union is made up of almost thirty different countries, each with its own laws, customs, and regulations which, like those in the US, are confusing and senseless, and often exist only so that politicians can be seen to be doing something. As in the US, enforcement of those laws and regulations is dependent on the decisions of the individual police officer or security person.

I've worked and traveled in Europe, Asia, and Latin America for decades, and lived mostly in Europe for the past ten years. I've written for *Blade* magazine and for *Knives*

Annual for almost twenty years and have written two books on knives: *The Tactical Knife*, and this, the second one, *Survival Knives*. As a result, I've met many folks in the European and international knife community, knifemakers, bushcraft enthusiasts, and so on. Also, I know many people who work in the security services and police departments in many European and other countries, and have talked with them about travelers carrying knives. What follows are my *personal experiences and opinions* based on traveling and living in almost every country in the European Union, and other countries not members of the Union, and in other parts of the world.

This is not meant to be an all-inclusive guide to the legalities of traveling with knives. It is, simply, what I can offer. I am not a lawyer. I offer no legal advice.

Some examples of regulations concerning knives in Europe and other places:

In Germany a person may not carry on his person any folding knife with a locking blade. These are considered to be weapons of hooligans. A person can, however, carry on his person a fixed blade up to three and one-half inches, which is not considered to be a hooligan's weapon.

In France a person may not carry on his person any object that could be, or is, used as a weapon. That means all knives, including France's famous Opinel and Laguiole knives, which are national icons and which are in the pockets of every third Frenchman, and are illegal if carried, even if only used to spread pâté at a picnic. Hair spray, keychains, purses, umbrellas, books, or anything with which you whack or poke an assailant would be considered a defensive weapon and therefore illegal. According to French law, you may only use verbal means to defend yourself.

Spain has considerable history as a knife culture and has knives of all kinds available for purchase pretty much every place, including village bars—and a confusing morass of regulations that vary from region to region, and that my friends who are Spanish police officers cannot understand or explain.

In the UK there was a recent attempt to prohibit chef's knives from having points. That regulation did not pass. My understanding of the current UK laws is that you must have a reason to have a knife, such as being a carpenter. Locking folders are not allowed. Bushcrafters with fixed blades on the way to do some bushcraft seem to get a pass.

In Denmark a person may not have any folding knife with a blade lock or which opens with one hand. Wait! That regulation was just changed. Locking folders are now okay, for today.

Attitudes about knives also vary by region. Eastern Europe, the Balkans, and Turkey are much more liberal about knives than Western Europe.

What's a traveler to do? How could anyone know or conform to all the different laws and regulations while traveling through four or five countries? You cannot. So, you have two choices: 1.) Do not have a knife, or 2.) Use some common sense. You can stop reading now if you select choice number one. If you want to know about choice number two, keep reading.

ML (my wife and companion of many adventures) and I always travel in Europe (and everyplace else) with knives, at least two each, often more. We frequently rent holiday apartments and live for a month or so in various places where we shop, cook, and settle in to experience local life. The kitchens in those apartments *never* have useable knives. We also like to camp, and on occasion we teach survival and bushcraft classes during which we make shelters, primitive tools, and so on. During the past few years I've been attacked by feral dog packs in the Balkans. On one occasion I had no stick and my knife was my only defense. Often I'm toting a half dozen or so knives in my luggage, ones that I'm reviewing for various publications. We need our knives.

Many Americans we meet traveling in Europe also need their knives. In addition to the practical everyday uses of a knife and its indispensable use in disasters, a blade can provide steely comfort in a dark and lonely place, and not only from dog packs. A young American woman, a solo world traveler I wrote about in my recent book, *Essential Survival Gear*, used her Henckels paring knife for daily camp chores while hiking in coastal mountains in Turkey, and was glad to have her little blade one night when a crowd of drunken men made her very uncomfortable. A retired American I met in Romania used his Benchmade 710 to cut the fuel line on his BMW motorcycle when the engine was running wild and would not stop, and for frequent picnics, and one dark night to confront two muggers, who decided to find easier prey. Potentially violent incidents like this are rare. Europe is in general safe for travelers. But hey, times are changing and you never know.

How do I and other folks travel in and through European and other countries with knives and not run afoul of the law? By using common sense. By being sensible in our selection of knives. By not doing stupid things such as going to some sketchy bar, getting drunk, hitting on a local girl and, when her boyfriend, also drunk, forcefully objects, waving a knife around and threatening him. Last year in Spain I saw three guys passing a bottle of wine and a folding knife around, cutting bread and cheese while picnicking at the beach. All good. Except they were talking loudly, arguing with each other, and annoying the folks around them. When one fellow politely objected to their behavior, one of these idiots grabbed the knife, shook it at the follow who had spoken to him, and yelled, "Allah Akbar!" Then he collapsed laughing, as did his friends. This incident didn't end well. Personal demeanor, behavior, and appearance will affect how you are perceived and treated by security people, and everyone else—not only in Europe but in every place in our world.

As to knife selection, attitudes in Western Europe regarding knives and security have changed considerably in recent years due to many terrorist attacks, some of which have been carried out with knives. As a consequence, although not yet common, there are security checks in some Western European train and bus stations, and of course in all airports. We've not yet encountered a security check at an Eastern European train or bus station. If you encounter one of these security checks, having a black, ten-inch bladed knife with saw teeth and Zombie Killer etched on it stuffed into your waistband will not endear you to security people.

When ML and I travel, in Western Europe or elsewhere, we each always have a tiny folder with a locking blade of about two inches on our persons and a small fixed blade in our bags. These knives look inoffensive and have caused no alarms with security people or anyone else. Folders with blades a bit larger, single blade or multi-blade such as small SAKs, have also been judged as inoffensive and acceptable. Most regulations address carrying a knife on the person as opposed to in a bag. Security people also seem to see a difference between carrying on your person and in a bag. Maybe not in all instances, but this has been our experience. I've never seen a knife in a day-bag with bread and cheese and other picnic things cause concern, mine or those belonging to others.

Our tiny folders are for everyday tasks, sometimes including food preparation when we don't care to get out our fixed blades. ML can girdle a baguette and reduce it to slices in less than a minute with her Spyderco Cricket. My Spyderco Dragonfly will slice salami, cheese, tomatoes, and so on about as well as my fixed blade. They will also serve in an emergency, if you know what you're doing. These little folders or others in the same size range or a bit larger are convenient everyday knives. The fixed blades we use in our kitchens, for field work, and for emergent situations. I also carry a small red-handled SAK with a locking main blade and the all-important corkscrew. We add to this selection if needed—say, a machete in the tropics.

Our day bags are also our ready bags, or bug-out bags, and are always with us. (How to travel the world with only a day bag and fifteen pounds of gear, and be prepared for anything, is the subject of my recent book, *Essential Survival Gear*.) Our fixed blades have much daily utility and will serve in an emergency, such as having to cut through a locked steel fire door to escape a high-rise fire, serve as a climbing aid to escape freezing water, or fend off a pack of feral dogs. At one time or another over the years I've done all these things, and know that if needed our fixed blades will provide us with a measure of security and protection.

We've only been questioned about our knives during a few security checks. Before boarding a high-speed train in Barcelona, we put our bags through the x-ray and walked through the metal detector. One of the security people asked if I had a knife. I said I did. He asked to see it. I first took out my Spyderco Dragonfly, intending to next get my Fällkniven F1 out of my bag. The security guy looked at the little Dragonfly, smiled, and said, 'Oh never mind. It's so little. Just put it back in your pocket.' He waved us through and said nothing about my F1, or ML's Spyderco Cricket and Fred Perrin Street Beat. Clearly, he made his evaluation based on our appearance and behavior as well as our choice of knives. On another occasion, while disembarking from a bus in Lyon, France, we encountered an intensive security check due to an alert that a terrorist suspect might be on our bus. Results were the same as in Barcelona, as they have been on other occasions. European police, like American police, evaluate the person and the situation when making a decision. We do not appear to be a threat, nor do our knives. When asked, we give a straightforward explanation of why we have knives, and have had no problems.

In Eastern Europe, the Balkans, and Turkey, attitudes concerning knives are *very* different. Full-size tactical folders are popular for everyday carry and no one seems alarmed by them.

Fixed blades, six to ten inches in blade length, are preferred for field activities, hunting, backpacking, and so on, and for use in villages to do everyday village things, such as killing pigs. I asked a friend, who is a Bulgarian undercover cop, what the laws were governing carrying knives in Bulgaria, and what the police attitude was. I also explained the regulations in Western Europe. He said, "We don't concern ourselves with such silly things. We don't care what kind of knife you have. But, if someone attacks and harms another person with a knife, or any weapon, then we do care." A former Czech special forces officer now in a civilian security service told me much the same thing.

We've only been questioned about knives in the East once, at Ataturk Airport in Istanbul. Going through first-layer security at the entrance to the airport, I tossed a bag onto the x-ray conveyor. It contained a kindjal, a yatagan, a ten-inch Bowie, and a half dozen or so tactical folders and fixed-blade survival knives, all for field work and photography for articles and books.

The security guy said, "You have quite a few knives in your bag."

▲ One of the author's Randal Model One knives.

"Yes," I said, "I do."

"You're going to check them, not carry them on, right?"

"Of course."

"Have a nice day."

Attitudes and laws concerning knives, and weapons, vary a great deal in Asian countries, and have changed over time. Back in the seventies I traveled throughout Southeast Asian countries with a handgun and at least one knife. I recall when the first metal detectors were installed in airports in Southeast Asia which was, to the best of my memory, about 1975 or 1976. Once during that period, I entered Manila from another Southeast Asian country and passed through customs and security at the international airport without question. The same day, when going through security at the domestic terminal prior to boarding a flight to a southern island, the newly installed metal detector sounded off when I walked through it. The security guard asked me if I was carrying a weapon.

"Yes," I replied.

"May I please see it?"

I cleared my pistol and handed it to him. I did not volunteer the six-inch bladed Randall Model One in its slip sheath in my waistband. Didn't seem important.

The guard looked closely at my handgun, turning it over and reading the manufacturer's mark.

"Ah, a Walther. A German gun, is it?"

"Yes, it is."

"Very nice. German guns are top quality."

He called another guard to come and admire my pistol. After they examined it, and after we talked about guns and about my travel plans for a few minutes, he returned my pistol.

I loaded it and put it back in its holster and went on to board the aircraft. To this day I'm not sure of the purpose of this security check. Was it simply an opportunity to examine passenger's weapons? Possibly by taking time to examine my firearm and talking with me, the guards determined that I presented no threat. Given the nature of the war in the Philippines at that time, the latter makes a bit more sense than the former. In any event, times have changed. These days I would not even consider international travel with a firearm, unless I was affiliated with an appropriate organization. Knives can also sometimes be a problem.

In Japan it is illegal to carry any knife on your person. Knives in checked baggage might be seized by customs officials. My knives were once taken by customs officials at Narita Airport and I never saw them again.

Singapore has strict prohibitions against bringing any knife into the country. On one occasion in the nineties a customs official politely informed me that I would have to leave my folder in their office. He gave me a receipt and I was able to retrieve my knife when I departed. While in Singapore I purchased a perfectly useable six-inch bladed fixed blade, which, along with every imaginable description of knife, was available in street markets. I've never been examined by customs officials when entering Cambodia or Vietnam.

I've never been questioned about my knives when entering Thailand or, in the old days, about my firearm. All manner of knives are available from every street corner vendor in Thailand. A word of caution: Contrary to what most tourists think, Thailand is a very violent country. Street crime is common, as are attacks on persons, including *farangs*—foreigners. There is considerable dislike of *farangs* among many Thai people. Tourists disappear every year in the 'Land of Smiles.' My short story, *Bangkok Blues*, available on Amazon, is a true account of some of my experiences in Bangkok.

Latin American countries also vary a good deal in their official approach to travelers with knives. Generally speaking, due to levels of endemic violence, Mexico and Guatemala consider all knives carried by travelers to be *armas blancas*, rather than tools, and will confiscate them and possibly jail the person carrying them. Often a "fine" can be paid on the spot to avoid jail. Violence is so rife in El Salvador that I would not travel there without a local contact and a firearm. I've not experienced or heard of travelers having problems with their knives in Costa Rica. There are, however, dozens of disappearances each year in Costa Rica. Violence in Brazil and other South American countries are at levels not commonly understood by Americans. As a result, virtually all knives carried by travelers throughout Latin America are considered to be *armas blancas*. Exceptions being bush travel, camping, and similar activities.

The decision to take or not take a knife with you on an international or cross-country journey is an individual one that should be made by considering all the pros and cons. In decades of world travel in over forty countries, I've never traveled without a knife. My choice is due to my background, my experiences, my activities, and my personal philosophy. I do not advocate that you do as I do. You must make your own choices.

Obviously, these days we check all knives before boarding a commercial aircraft. We are polite when dealing with police or security people, as we are with all people. Your attitude will have a great deal to do with how you are treated. If you choose to take a knife or knives, select those that are not likely to alarm people, such as those I mentioned earlier. Avoid black blades, even if the black coating is only meant to retard corrosion. Black blades just *look* like weapons rather than tools. If you like to drink and hang out in sketchy bars and clubs, leave your knife in your room. Don't try to use your knife as a weapon, except in extreme circumstances when your own life is actually at stake. Doing so is considered lethal force everywhere and you will have to defend your actions. Again, use common sense. You have an internal compass that points in the right direction. Pay attention to it. This approach has worked for us. Your results may vary. No guarantee is offered or implied.

Conclusion—Using Survival Knives

My purpose in writing this book is to save lives. In fact, saving lives has been my goal in writing each book in this series. I've witnessed too many lives lost for want of a simple tool, a little knowledge, and a measure of caution. In truth, one was too many.

One of my friends told me that, given the life I have led, advising others to be cautious seems contradictory. But that's not so if we take a closer look. By some standards I've led, and still lead, an adventurous life. As a child and teenager, I wandered wilderness on my own, hitchhiked across three states, hopped freight trains across the country, climbed the outside of ten- and twelve-story brick buildings, and, with Huck Finn as inspiration, made a raft and floated downriver on it for a week. I've jumped from airplanes, climbed mountains, explored uncharted jungles, lived with what the developed world considers primitive people, and sailed five of the seven seas in small boats to islands where the only light came from the sun, moon, and fire, and the only food came from the sea. I did all of these things before instant worldwide communication and when the notion of traveler's health insurance was laughable. In those days, when you went to a remote place, you were damn well there, and responsible for getting out of whatever trouble you might get into. Still, well into my seventh decade, I wander the world and greet each day as an adventure.

I've even done the most challenging things anyone can do, the things most of you have done: earning a living and raising a family. And, like most of you, I learned that my children were hostages to fate. I did all I knew how to do to prepare my children for our wonderful, terrible, world—and taught them the skills in these books, the most important one being to listen to the advice fear provides but to never allow fear to control them.

In all these activities, I've never been careless. Caution, forethought, preparedness, all these are hallmarks of the paratrooper, the explorer, the survivor. A paratrooper trains for weeks before his first jump. Like your maiden aunt preparing for a trip to the mall, he checks his equipment, once, twice, three times. He checks his buddy's equipment and his buddy checks his. His jump master checks all equipment. Only after acquiring the necessary skills, only after learning each piece of equipment and its use, and only after checking and rechecking each item does he jump from an aircraft while in flight. Even then he doesn't *know* his parachute will open. That's why he has a reserve.

Each day we live is much like a parachute jump. Each day we awaken without knowing if we will be alive to see the sunset. Somewhere deep in the recesses of our minds and hearts we all know that sunset is not promised to all who see sunrise. Some choose to ignore this reality and go through life half awake. Others face death, accept it as an advisor, find freedom, and go through life fearlessly and fully engaged.

Read *The Tao of Survival* to learn mind/body skills, self-healing and health, hyper-awareness and how to avoid threats and better perceive the magic and wonder of our world, and learn how to make fear your ally. Like fire, fear is a good servant and a bad master. *Essential Survival Gear* teaches minimalism and simplicity in material things and how to equip yourself for any contingency. The core lessons in *Survival Knives* are these: Have a knife. Know how to use it.

The most important lesson in all of these books: Live life fully, have fun, go where your heart takes you, but be ready for whatever may come.

Chapter Ten

Recommended Survival Knives and Their Makers

This is not an exhaustive directory of all available survival knives. Nor have I attempted to include all the knives from all knifemakers I have reviewed during the twenty years or so I've been writing about knives. New knife models are introduced each year and old models go out of production. A book such as this cannot stay current with knifemakers' output. Instead, I recommend knifemakers who have over a period of time been proven to make reliable, good-quality knives. I've included some knives that are not billed as survival knives, but are good-quality knives that can fulfill the "have it with you" function. In some cases, I comment on one or two of their classic models, ones that have been in production for some time and are likely to remain in production. Some of these makers and their knives have also been mentioned in *The Tactical Knife*.

Testing Survival Knives

Each of the knives I recommend have been used under field conditions by my associates and myself, and often by our students, sometimes over a period of years. We test survival knives, and all knives, as they are meant to be used in the field. To test cutting ability for self-defense, we utilize various cutting tests used when I was training in Silat in Bali and in Escrima/Kali in Cebu, Philippines. Some of the tests are used by The American Bladesmith Society (ABS). The ABS tests include cutting tissue paper, free hanging hemp rope, and chopping 2x4s. One of the tests from Escrima is to wrap a piece of flank steak around a length of bamboo, to simulate muscle and bone, then wrap the steak with a thin towel and very light cotton fabric to simulate clothing, then hang this bundle from a tree limb and slash it.

For knives billed as hard use, we drive them into trees and do a few pull ups on them, stab hard wood and rip out chunks of wood with the point, pry apart wood that has been nailed together, cut and stab sheet metal, and, using the spine of the blade, deconstruct brick and concrete block walls.

You might want to try some of things yourself. If so, do them with care, for the possibility of injury is real. I accept no responsibility for any injury that might occur, or for any damage to your knife. Undertaking such testing can lead to personal injury, and doing so, is your decision alone. Also, such testing might destroy a knife. We have seen many knives fail over the years, some catastrophically. My view is that if a knife is to fail, better that it do so during practice than during survival conditions. We also use a large measure of common sense. If a knife is not advertised as a hard-use knife, we do not test it as such. In no case would we try to do pull-ups on a folder. We do not deliberately test to destruction.

Al Mar Knives
P.O. Box 2295
Tualatin, OR 97062
www.almarknives.com

Al Mar Knives was founded by Al Mar, a former special forces soldier and talented knife designer.

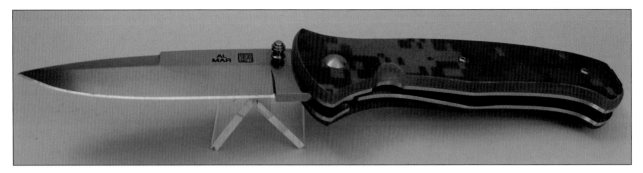

▲ Al Mar SERE.

The company founder passed away some years ago, but the company that bears his name continues. Al worked with Colonel "Nick" Rowe, a special forces officer who survived seven years of captivity by the Viet Cong, and who founded the US Army's Survival Escape Resistance and Evasion (SERE) school, to design the SERE folder. This was the first folder purpose-designed as a survival knife, and was meant to be worn on the person, rather than in load-bearing gear as large fixed blades are carried by soldiers

The original SERE, a massive folder, is no longer in production. The SERE 2000, a smaller and in some ways improved model, has stood up to hard use by many of my inexperienced students. The liner lock is solid and remains so even after they have used it to construct shelters with the use of a baton, which qualifies as hard use. The SERE 2000 suffered no damage of any kind during some weeks of use by a variety of students. The 3.6-inch blade is a modified spear point made of VG-10 and is useful for a wide range of tasks. The scales are textured G-10. The comment most often heard about the SERE 2000 is that it's comfortable in the hand even after hours of work.

Benchmade Knives

300 Beavercreek Rd.
Oregon City, OR 97045
(800) 800–7427
www.benchmade.com

Benchmade is an industry leader, well known for innovation and quality. Over the years I have found that they make a wide range of top-quality knives and provide exemplary service.

The Benchmade 710 was the first folder to utilize the Axis Lock, a Benchmade innovation generally considered to be one of the strongest folder locks developed. The 710, with its four-inch blade, comfortable handle, and reliable lock, has over many years of production become an industry icon. My associates and I, and our students, have used 710s in the field for over fifteen years. We've batoned them, built shelters in wilderness,

▲ Benchmade Model 710.

dressed game, and sliced bread in France with them. One of the top half-dozen or so folders for survival use. Excellent knife, no reservations.

Benchmade's Nimravus is a fixed blade with a four- and one-half-inch blade tough enough to scrape through a cinderblock wall or field dress a Honda. The overall length of 9.45 inches makes for a compact package, and its weight of only 6.2 ounces is lighter than some folders. This is a compact, tough, handy fixed blade. The blade geometry works in the kitchen, when dressing game, carving wood, and the above-mentioned extreme tasks, as well as others such as pounding into a tree and using it as weight-bearing device. You could probably rip open the door of a stuck elevator with it. Its only disadvantage is its black blade, which makes it appear to be more of a weapon than a tool and causes consternation from customs officials and the general public.

The Benchmade Bushcrafter is about the same size and at least as strong at the Nimravus, and much friendlier in appearance. Its "Scandi" edge is preferred by many bushcrafters and outdoors people. You'll want a diamond hone to keep its S30V blade sharp. This is a tough fixed blade suitable for hard use as well as bushcrafting. We stabbed it into seasoned oak and ripped it out, and punched through sheet metal with no damage.

Böker USA Inc.

1550 Balsam Street
Lakewood, CO 80214
(800) 835–6433
www.bokerusa.com

Böker is an old-line Solingen Germany knife company, which was founded under a chestnut tree in the seventeenth century. The company makes a wide range of knives. The Böker Plus Subcom by Chad los Banos is a frame-lock folder the size of a business card. Its clip serves as a money clip, or to secure it to clothing. This is a nice little knife suitable for the uses discussed in Hideout Knives at an affordable price.

Buck Knives

660 South Lochsa Street
Post Falls, ID 83854–52000
(800) 326–2825
www.buckknives.com

A family company founded in 1902 by Hoyt Buck, a young blacksmith, Buck Knives has become an American institution.

With more than forty years of production behind it, the Buck 110 folding Hunter, with its lockback and exceptional edge holding, has become an American icon. Lacking the modern features of a pocket clip or a one-handed blade

▲ Buck Compadre notching a bow stave.

opener, it is still a solid serviceable knife that many outdoorsmen carry—and so has been and likely will continue to be used as a survival knife. The current Buck range of knives includes a number of knives suitable for survival.

Bud Nealy Knifemaker

RR 1, Box 1439
Stroudsburg, PA 18360
(570) 402–1018
www.budnealyknifemaker.com

Bud Nealy is widely recognized as one of the top rank of knifemakers in the world. Bud is also famous in certain circles for making some of the finest fixed blades available for covert operators, clandestine agents, and military and law enforcement personal. His patented sheath system, the MCS (Multi-Concealment Sheath), is unseen by many, and in use, along with his knives, by people in the previously mentioned occupations as well as S.W.A.T and R.A.I.D teams, US embassy guards, EMT personal, reporters, NGO workers, and other international travelers who work in dangerous environments. Nealy's knives are tough, effective, and purpose designed. They are also little gems

▲ Bud Nealy fixed blade cutting hemp rope.

made with such craft, grace, and style that on first viewing you might think they're too nice to actually use. Any of them will serve as a small survival knife.

Busse Combat Knife Co.

11651 County Rd. 12
Wauseon, OH 43567
(419) 923–6471
www.bussecombat.com

Busse uses steel they call INFI and claim as proprietary, as well as a heat-treat method they also identify as proprietary. They attribute many virtues to this steel, including the ability to bend to thirty-five degrees and to spring back to true, along with edge retention and an absence of edge damage in hard use.

I don't know anything about INFI steel, but I do know from experience that the Busse Steel Heart I used cut through an auto body like it was tinfoil, and that there was no damage to the edge or blade after doing so. Over a period of a few weeks we used the Steel Heart for about anything you would use a big knife for. It was tough. It stayed sharp. With a nine-inch blade with the balance forward and quite a bit of belly, it was a good chopper.

▲ Busse Utility Knife.

Chris Reeve Knives

2949 S. Victory View Way
Boise, ID 83709
(208) 375–0367
www.chrisreeve.com

Over the past decade I've put in many hours using Chris Reeve knives to demonstrate survival techniques, and I've loaned Chris Reeve knives to many of my students. I have never once seen a poorly made Chris Reeve knife or one that failed to perform as advertised.

Chris Reeve is best known for his iconic Sebenza. It's a folder that embodies minimalist industrial chic and is as much a work of modern art as it is a functional knife. I once saw a new student swing his baton at a Sebenza like he was trying for a home run. No damage. One kid used a Sebenza and a baton to cut enough saplings for a four-person shelter in about twenty minutes of non-stop cutting and tapping. The knife went through saplings like they were butter.

Chris Reeve also makes the official knife awarded to those who graduate today's Q Course at the Special Warfare Center. It's known to the US Army Special Forces as "The Yarborough" and to everyone else as "The Green Beret Knife." As you might imagine of a knife that was selected by active duty serving SF soldiers, the Green Beret Knife and its smaller brother will do anything a special warfare

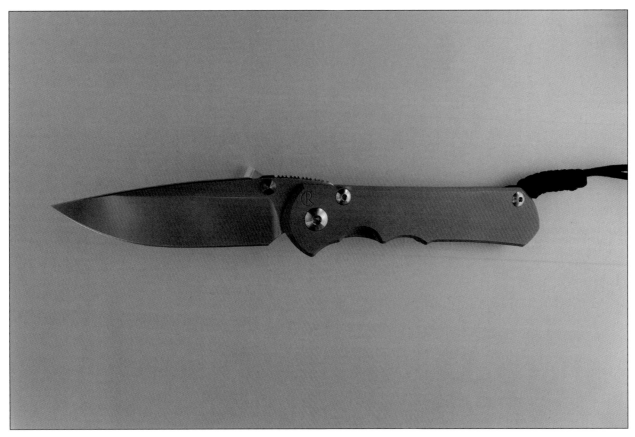

▲ Chris Reeve Sebenza.

operator could expect of a knife. Available with either a seven-inch or 5.5-inch blade of KG Gun-Koted CPMS30V, the knives were designed by well-known knifemaker and designer Bill Harsey, with function and manufacturing input from Chris Reeve. A civilian version, without a serial number, is also available. My students and I tried out the seven-inch version over an extended period. It's a good knife.

The Professional Soldier, also designed in collaboration with Bill Harsey for a group of SF soldiers, is a small, solid, deceptively simple-looking one-piece, flat-frame fixed blade. With its 3.3-inch blade and an overall length of seven and one-half inches, it is small enough, and light enough at three ounces, to tuck into a pocket, a sock, or just about anywhere. Mine arrived sharp enough to easily shave hair and stayed reasonably sharp even after work on hard woods as well as the usual stuff: cutting sheetrock to size, slicing tomatoes, and so on.

This is a well-conceived, well-designed, and well-made little knife, an actual working blade as opposed to a "use it only in an emergency" knife, and a very slick hideout survival knife.

Cold Steel Inc.

3036-A Seaborg Ave.
Ventura, CA 93003
(800) 255–4716
www.coldsteel.com

Three Cold Steel knives that we've used and can recommend for survival are the SRKs (Survival Rescue Knife), the Trail Master Bowie, and the Laredo Bowie.

I gave a Laredo to a young friend, a survival student, and asked him to try it out. He used it during the three or four days we spent together in coastal mountains. He also used some other knives I had brought along to review. On our way home, I asked him *the question*, "Which knife would you chose, out of all these knives, if you could only have one knife?" Then I put conditions on it. "You'll be in the mountains for a month and will have to provide everything for yourself." After thoughtful pause, he said, "It would have to be that Bowie (Laredo). It would save time. I could make a shelter and get firewood in like . . . 10 percent of the time it would take with a little knife. And the point is good enough to skin a squirrel. Besides, no one who sees me in the mountains would freak out at its size, like they would in town."

Columbia River Knife & Tool (CRKT)

18348 SW 126th Place
Tualatin, OR 97062
(800) 891–3100
www.crkt.com

The M16 series, designed by Kit Carson—yes, that's his real name—is one of the most popular knives sold to active-duty soldiers, and for good reason. Well designed and well executed to be an everyday tool and emergency weapon, every model is this series is exactly that. Its liner lock is doubly secured by its "Lawks" system. The troops use them for everything from opening boxes, packages, and MREs (Meals Ready to Eat—three lies in one name, according to the troops) to cutting rope and nylon strapping, and carry them all the time. Since they carry them all the time, they are available as emergency weapons. A knife in this series was the one used by the Marine I wrote about in *"Death Among the Reeds,"* in The *Tactical Knife*. Obviously, if

▲ M16 breaking through a door frame.

the M16 tactical folder saved one Marine's life, it can save another's, or anyone's. I am sometimes asked by active-duty service people to recommend a knife that fits the following criteria: a folder so it's convenient to have on their person all times; tough enough to stand up to generally harsh field use; designed so that it can be used as a weapon if needed; and affordable on an enlisted man's salary. The M16 series is the one I most often recommend. I've used a number of the M16 series over the years and have no reservations recommending them. One of the top half dozen folding knives suitable for survival use.

Columbia River Knife & Tool also makes a wide range of good quality and good value folders and fixed blades, many of them suitable for survival use, including a new model in the M16 Series with a blade that measures only three inches, which is legal in most places. The Japanese styled smallish fixed blades designed by Lucas Burnley are very handy and would serve as 'have it with you' fixed blades.

Daniel Winkler Knives

P.O. Box 2166
Blowing Rock, NC 26605
(828) 295–9156
www.winklerknives.com

Daniel Winkler occupies a unique place in tactical cutlery today in that he is the only ABS Mastersmith I know of who has for years specialized in knives and tomahawks of the Colonial Period. Now, under the Winkler II brand, he is bringing that expertise and consciousness to the creation of war-ready knives for the special operations community.

The two most popular Winkler II models with the special operations community are the WKII Belt Knife and the WKII Field Knife. We've used and tested both for over five years, cutting everything from rope to sheet metal, prying open locked doors, batoning them, and stabbing them into seasoned oak and twisting and ripping them out. The Field Knife has a 5 ¾-inch blade and measures ten and one-half inches overall. The Belt Knife comes in a little shorter, with a four and one-half-inch blade and 8 ¾-inch overall length. I like both of these knives very much. The designs are sensible. The flat ground blades do not hang up in wood, and they cut through meat as well as kitchen knives. Tough knives, they will serve as survival and E&E tools as well as any commercially available knives I am aware of, and better than most. They are well balanced for use as weapons. The non-slip grips do not in fact slip, even when hands are wet or slippery. In short, they are excellent all-around knives for special operators, or anyone who lives life on the edge and might need a knife to keep him from going over.

DPX

dpxgear.com
(888) 233–3924

The H.E.S.T. (Hostile Environment Survival Tool) was DPXs first product. Designed by Robert Young Pelton, the well-known author of *The World's Most Dangerous Places*, and other books, the H.E.S.T. is a small, 7 5/8-inch overall fixed blade, of 3/8-inch-thick carbon steel, and with a number of features that I was not so sure about at first: a wire beaker, a bottle opener, and a mini pry bar on the butt. Generally speaking, I'm not a fan of multipurpose knives, except for the SAK, which I view as a small toolbox rather than a knife. Also, I was concerned that the bottle opener, which is a notch on top of the blade, would make for a stress riser and lead to blade failure. To test that hypothesis, one of my younger students obliged me by trying out the H.E.S.T. as a climbing device. After stabbing the point into a pine tree, he levered himself upwards into the lower branches. No problem. Wanting to try something a little harder, he batoned the blade into the tree trunk about two inches, then put all of his 175 pounds on the lateral plane and walked up the side of the tree. No problem. The blade did flex at the bottle opener notch but went back to true as soon as his weight was removed. We've now used the original H.E.S.T for almost ten years. We like it. It's well balanced, comfortable in hand, and useful for a wide range of tasks, including ripping open a door in a building scheduled for demolition, hacking through sheetrock, and slicing tomatoes. I keep a little cash and a flint stick under the scales in its hollow recess. DPX now makes a folding version of the H.E.S.T (and a full range of fixed blade and folders) that's about as strong as technology will allow a folder to be made today. I wouldn't suggest that anyone to try and do pull-ups on the folder, but it's in the top rank and about as good as it gets for a folding survival knife.

ESEE Knives

P.O. Box 99
Gallant, AL 35972
Phone: (256) 613–0372
email: info@eseeknives.com

Mike Perrin and Jeff Randall, the honchos of ESEE Knives, use 1095 carbon steel for all

▲ ESEE Izula with Indonesian bow and arrow case.

their knives. With one of the best heat treats in the industry, they make strong blades that will flex under hard stress without breaking and spring back to true. Best known for their Izula, a small fixed blade usually characterized as a "neck knife," the Izula is supplied with a sheath that has a spring clip, and so can be clipped to clothing (which I prefer) as well as worn around the neck with the supplied ball chain. Every ESEE knife, and there is a large range of them, that we have used has been a good example of what a survival knife should be.

Fällkniven AB

Granatvagen 8
961 43 BODEN
www.fallkniven.se

U.S. Distributor

Blue Ridge Knives
166 Adwolfe Road
Marion, VA 24354–6664
(276) 783–6143
www.blueridgeknives.com

The Fällkniven F1, S1, and A1, are some of the best purpose-designed survival knives in production today. The Fällkniven line up is quite large and includes everything from a small but comfortable-to-work-with "neck knife" to large Bowies. Every model in the product range has the same design sensibility and commitment to function. The quality of manufacturing is top level. I have never seen a poorly conceived or poorly made Fällkniven. Over the years I have found these three Fällkniven knives to

be not only functional for a wide variety of knife work, but exceptional in performance as survival knives. They each have convex grinds, excellent ergonomics, and blade geometry, and excel at everything from bushcraft to deconstructing brick walls.

The F1, being the smallest, is the easiest to carry and fulfills the "have it with you" standard. It was selected as the issue survival knife for the Swedish Air Force and has been approved by the US Navy as a pilot's survival knife. Since the F1's introduction in 1995, it has become the standard—a very high standard—to which all small survival knives are compared. The S1 is a bit larger and stronger, but still fits in an aviator's survival vest, and perhaps into your waistband. The A1, with its thick six-inch blade, is the big dog of the pack. Too large for an aviator's vest, it is the issue knife for certain units of the Russian army, and has been approved by the US military. During the last few months I've been using a Fällkniven F1 Pro, a new version of an old favorite. Other than the guard, the improvements are subtle, but significant. The blade is a bit thicker, the grind is slightly different. There's a clip point instead of a drop point. The Pro Series (there's now also an S1 Pro and A1 Pro) comes nicely packaged in a waterproof box, and with an excellent field sharpener, diamond on one side, stone on the other. The F1 Pro cuts and performs at the top of its class and sets a new standard. It's an excellent, small enough to have at all times survival knife. I've used Fällkniven survival knives for over fifteen years and recommend them without reservation.

▲ Fällkniven F1 Pro.

Fred Perrin

La Gare
71390 Jully les Buxy
France

Fred Perrin is a former French army commando, a national tae kwon do champion, all-Europe full-contact stick-fighting champion, and a master of savate, hardcore, full-contact French kick boxing. Fred has considerable real-world experience.

Fred is well known in the States for his production and semi-production knives, including the Spyderco Street Beat and Street Bowie, two of the best designed and executed fixed blades available today, and others from his own production, including the La Griffe, the Shark, and the Neck Bowie. Designed as weapons suited for the modern world, these knives are also graceful, elegant, well made, and tough. In addition to their self-defense function, they work well as all-around utility knives and will stand up to hard use and the rigors of survival.

As an example, the Shark is what Fred describes as "the smallest effective blade I could design." The slim sliver of steel fits in my wallet, or on a key ring. On a dog-tag chain carried around the neck, the Shark is almost as light as dog tags, barely noticeable. The large finger ring provides a quick and secure grip and, with its attached cord, makes for a surprisingly comfortable and effective grip. The tiny blade will cut a one-inch hanging rope, a test used by the American Bladesmith Society, and slash through four water-filled plastic bottles. It press cut through twenty-two layers of tightly rolled denim. It's a handy tool to open envelopes and boxes, cut rubber hose, and so on. I've used the Shark in the kitchen and found that it will slice

a flank steak into strips for barbecue as well as a kitchen knife will. I've also made arrows and fletched them with the Shark. It's a perfect example of the tiny, have-it-with-you blade.

While wandering along the Turkish coast, I used a Perrin Neck Bowie to make a fish trap from a discarded plastic water bottle by cutting off the tapered part of the top, slicing off the lid, and placing the resulting cone inside the bottle. Tuna scraps served as bait. I wedged the trap in place with rocks, opening facing the outgoing tide. While waiting for our fish trap to produce, we went foraging. The hills above the Mediterranean are covered with edible plants. Some require local knowledge to identify; others include familiar dandelion greens, rose hips, wild peppers, and prickly pear cactus. Prickly pear pads can be eaten raw in a salad, grilled, or cooked with tomatoes to make a delicious Mexican dish. While foraging, I used the Neck Bowie to cut shelter poles to make a tripod, secured a "space blanket" as a covering, then cut tall grass to cover the ground under our shelter with a foot-deep grass bed. When we returned to the water, we found two small fish in our trap. While anticipating the tasty dinner to come, we set up the results of our foraging for photos. However, as we fiddled with cameras, a feral cat crept up, snatched one of the fish, and made off with it. I almost fell from a slippery rock into the water laughing. Rather than chase the hungry cat away, we made a short video of the bold adventurer stealing the other fish. The video can be seen on my website. Deprived of our fish dinner, we fell back on emergency rations—a block of goat cheese and a bottle of white wine, which we had with the wild green salad at our little shelter while watching the sun sink into the sea.

◀ Fred Perrin Neck Bowie and CRKT Ken Onion design.

▲ Cat stealing fish.

Last year in Brittany we visited some friends who were remodeling an old, stone village house. I helped to deconstruct a stone wall with one of Fred's Mid-tech Bowies. By using the spine rather than the edge, and by working slowly, pressing rather than stabbing, no damage was done to the knife. Fred also hand forges custom knives, which are striking in appearance and performance. Most of Fred's blades tend toward small, and are so light you hardly notice you have them, until needed.

Elsa Fantino
La Gare
71390 Jully les Buxy
France

Elsa Fantino is a bladesmith whose stunning blades create their own aesthetic, a unique fusion of feminine art, power, and purpose. Medieval, otherworldly, or from a dream world, I've never before seen their like. If your imagination is captured by Elsa's work, as was mine,

▲ Collection of Elsa Fantino's knives.

be assured that these brilliantly designed and crafted blades are functional tools and weapons, not only creative craft. During cutting tests in the forest, we cut saplings for primitive shelters. Elsa's blades performed as a bladesmith's blades should perform: They cut well and efficiently, and held their edges. In the shop, Elsa's knives cut rope, thickly rolled fabric, and heavy cardboard with ease. Elsa used her "Avatar," a knife inspired by the film Avatar, and which has a blade like a giant raptor's claw and the bejeweled hilt and handle that characterizes most her work, to bring down saplings as easily as this blade would bring down a warrior princess's enemies. Elsa's work is new to most people on this side of the pond, but it won't be for long. Elsa is a rising star.

Gerber Legendary Blades

Gerber Gear
14200 SW 72nd Avenue
Portland, OR 97224
(800) 950–6161
www.gerbergear.com

Gerber Legendary Blades was launched by Joseph Gerber in 1939, and has been long known for making affordable, good-quality

▲ Bear Gryll's collection for Gerber Legendary Blades (left to right): fire starter, multitool, compact fixed blade, fixed blade, and compact parang.

knives. Gerber currently makes the Bear Grylls line of survival blades. Due to all the hype, I was skeptical of the Bear Grylls knives. However, much use over six or seven months proved these knives to be well designed for survival, highly functional, and affordable. We ripped through sheet rock, slashed sheet metal, and sliced tomatoes with these knives. They're good to go.

KA-BAR Knives Inc.

200 Homer St.
Olean, NY 14760
(716) 372- 5952
www.kabar.com

The KA-BAR company has manufactured the original KA-BAR design, which was adopted by the United States Marine Corp, since 1942. Today the basic KA-BAR, like its ancestors, still has a seven-inch Bowie-inspired clip-point blade of 1095 carbon steel and a 4 ¾-inch handle of stacked leather washers. The blade has a saber grind and has the same high degree of utility that it has always had. Many of our students have shown up for class with a new KA-BAR. None of our student's KA-BARs have failed, and that during some pretty hard use.

KA-BAR also produces a wide range of fixed blades and folders, at affordable prices, that are suitable for survival. The Becker Necker, made by KA-BAR, is an excellent little utility knife and emergency weapon, tough enough to stand up to hard use. We have batoned the Necker through hardwood and sheet metal and used it for everyday tasks. It took no damage from the hard use and, with its good blade design, was very efficient in the kitchen. Billed as a neck knife, it's also offered with a sheath with a clip, which is the way I would carry it.

Mora Knives

Industrial Revolution, Inc.
5835 Segale Park Drive C
Tukwila, WA 98188
1-888-297-6062
info@industrialrev.com

The basic Mora knife has been in use by the primitive skills community for over twenty years. Mora knives have good steel, both stainless and carbon. They're excellent cutters, and due to the "scandi" grind, are easy for the neophyte to sharpen. They excel at woodcraft, but are not strong enough for hard use, and I do not recommend them as all-around survival knives. Recently, Mora released the Garburg, a thick-bladed, full-tang knife with the virtues of the basic Mora, and the strength and versatility needed for a survival knife. We've been using a Garburg for two months and have found it to

▲ A collection of Mora knives.

be a good daily user with enough muscle for hard use.

Mykel Hawke Knives

www.mykelhawke.com

Mykel Hawke, the well-known star of "Man Woman Wild" and other television shows, is a retired special forces (Green Beret) officer who knows more about wilderness survival than just about anyone I know. He has put that expertise to good use in designing survival knives, and more recently a wide range of survival tools. We've used many of them. A folder and his signature model, The Peregrine, are standouts.

Mykel's knives are radical in appearance. The designs derived from his years of field experience. I tend toward the traditional in knives and was somewhat dubious when I first received a Peregrine. To my eye it looked like a Klingon war knife. However, my first few hours of use, drilling a fire board, sharpening an arrow, planing the flats on a throwing stick, and cutting meat and vegetables for soup, dispelled all doubts. The blade design of the folder is similar to the Peregrine. It too worked well for all these tasks. Over a period of a couple of months, we used the Peregrine while foraging in the desert, for making shelters in mountains, and for ripping through lath and plaster in urban areas. We used it hard—survival knife, right? It did not fail. It sharpened easily. The handle was one of the most comfortable for hard work I've ever used. Clearly Mykel has worked with many knives, drawn lessons from them, and incorporated those lessons into his knives. Mykel's knives are practical, hardworking, efficient survival tools. You can rely on them.

Murray Carter Master Bladesmith

Carter Cutlery
2038 NW Aloclek Drive, Suite #225
Hillsboro, Oregon 97124
(503) 466–1331
Email: Murray@CarterCutlery.com

We have used only one Murray Carter knife, the FS1, a hand-forged blade of Japanese steel, laminated and made in the tradition of Japanese swords. Murray studied and trained in Japan for many years under the tutelage of a Japanese sword maker of ancient linage. His FS1 shows that influence. It is an excellent cutting instrument. The FS1 is well designed, well balanced, nicely proportioned, finely finished, and cuts like a five-inch razor. It also stays sharp for a long time. We used the FS1 for about three weeks in the kitchen, and to split kindling and do some woodwork. During this time, we were testing a dozen or so knives for cutting ability and decided to include the FS1. The cutting tests included one we used when I was training in Escrima in Cebu, Philippines. We wrapped a piece of flank steak around a length of bamboo, to simulate muscle and bone, then wrapped the steak with a thin towel and very light, tissue-thin cotton fabric to simulate clothing. We hung his bundle from a tree limb and slashed it. The FS1 tied for top spot in terms of cutting ability with one other knife, which was also a forged custom blade. We also cut a couple of feet of one-inch hemp rope into slices, a task that will quickly dull most blades. I can't tell you how long the FS1 stays sharp because after all this use it will still shave hair. If the notion of having a sort of small Japanese sword that doubles as a utility knife tickles your fancy, you've found your heart's desire.

▲ Murray Carter FS1 Fixed Blade.

Ontario Knife Company

P.O. Box 145
Franklinville, NY 14737
(800) 222–5233
www.ontarioknife.com

Ontario has been in business since 1889 and is perhaps best known as a supplier of knives to the American military. Over the years they have produced the M7 bayonet, the Air Force Survival Knife, and many others. They are currently making the Aircrew Survival Egress Knife for aircrew. In addition, Ontario makes a wide variety of knives and edged tools, including machetes, swords, tactical folders, and their Spec Plus brand, which is military oriented. Ontario has also been a contractor for the U.S.M.C. fighting knife (KA-BAR) and for RAT knives. We have used many Ontario knives, including the Air Force Survival Knife and the Spec Plus range. They're all made from tried and proven 1095 carbon steel, with a good heat treat, and are all good, reliable survival knives.

Randall Made Knives

4857 South Orange Blossom Trail
Orlando, FL 32839
(407) 855–8075
www.randallknives.com

I wrote extensively about Randall Knives in *The Tactical Knife*. If you're interested in the history of Randall Knives in WW II, and their adaption by the special forces in the sixties, I refer you to that book. I used Randalls as survival and defensive knives for over thirty years and recommend them without reservation. However, Randalls have become collector's knives, and as a result are hard to come by and very expensive. If you can afford the price and don't mind waiting, you won't be disappointed. If you do get a Randall, for God's sake use it. Don't tuck it away in some squirrel cache.

Strider Knives

120 N. Pacific St. Unit L-7
San Marcos, CA 92069
(760) 471–8275
www.striderknives.com

Every Strider knife I have used, both folder and fixed blade, has been built with the highest level of craftsmanship and from premium materials. These knives are muscular and tough and come from the factory as sharp as Einstein's brain. They stay that way for a very long time, even after cutting through walls and steel doors.

I've had one of Strider's small fixed blades for almost ten years, about seven inches overall, slim Kydex sheath, small enough to stick in your pocket or waistband and carry daily, and it's just a beast. It's a little thick for food preparation but will dress out your rabbits and deer and will slice tomatoes, root vegetables, and so on. We used it to cut a hole in a Honda's roof and it didn't even ding the edge. It also ripped through a plaster wall, not wall board, lath, and plaster, and afterwards was sharp enough to sharpen an arrow and slice roast beef thin. Get a DMT credit-card-sized diamond hone to sharpen it, put it in your wallet, and you'll be good to go. This is your basic have-it with-you-all-the-time, end-of-the-world knife.

Spyderco Inc.

**820 Spyderco Way
Golden, CO 80403–8053
(800) 525–7770
www.spyderco.com**

Spyderco has many excellent designs. They're all well made of the best available materials, and many are suitable for survival use.

The Military is their classic tactical folder and one of the top survival-grade folders. The Military is so slender that it appears delicate. It is not delicate. It looks like a dancer but performs like a linebacker. I've loaned my Military to my survival students and watched them baton their way through dozens of wrist-thick saplings to make shelters with no damage to the knife, using correct technique of course. One, and only one, caution: The tip is thin, so you don't want to stab into hardwood and snap it out sideways. I've used the Military for all manner of rough outdoor work for over fifteen years. With its flat ground four-inch blade, it's also a fine everyday tool, in the kitchen or elsewhere. The blade slips through ribs and roasts like cutting whipped cream. They come sharp from the factory and are easy to keep sharp. I *always* have at least one knife to hand. Due to its feather weight and slim configuration, and because I know I can rely on it, the Military is often *it*. I clip it inside my running shorts when I drag myself away from the keyboard for a mind-calming run. Closed, it's a little long at five- and one-half inches. Open, it's nine- and one-half inches overall. If I hold it at the butt of the handle, which I can do comfortably and securely, it gives me about five and a half to six inches reach, which is longer than the average

feral dog's snout. I'm sure of this. I usually have a Military in my bag when I check it at the airport.

With its three-inch blade, and only four inches closed, and with its Integral lock and RotoBlock secondary locking device, one of Spyderco's new models, the Lil Lion, makes an almost perfect pocket-sized folding survival knife. The blade is thick for a folder, which gives it extra strength, and has an excellent convex grind from spine to edge, which gives it superior cutting ability. The blade has plenty of belly for slicing and slashing, the point penetrates well and is well supported. We've been using a Lil Lion for a few months, made a bow and a couple of spears, drilled a fire-board, sliced pounds of beef and lamb, tomatoes, potatoes, and so on, cut up a knee-high stack of heavy cardboard, about ten feet of one-inch hemp rope, and then, after all that, we only had to strop it on a ceramic stone ten times on each side to bring the edge back to hair-shaving sharp. I think this is a good one, a very good one.

We've been using Spyderco's Fred Perrin Street Beat, a small knife designed by the well-known French designer, martial artist, and veteran of special operations for years. The Street Beat has a smooth, functional flat-grind three- and one-half-inch blade, comfortable handle, clean design, excellent quality, and a reserve of strength that is not immediately apparent. To demonstrate what could be done with a top-quality, well-designed small knife, I made a survival shelter with it in the middle of a Bulgarian snowstorm, and punched it through a plaster wall with no damage. Students were impressed. A few years ago, I used it to jimmy open the thick door of a chateau, as we had

▲ Spyderco Lil Lion.

the wrong security code. The Perrin Street Beat looks like a polite picnic knife and will slice your baguette and spread your Brie without raising an eyebrow. It will also do whatever needs to be done to help you survive. ML got a look at my Street Beat and snatched it so fast I didn't see her hand move. Now it's her favorite kitchen knife. She always packs *her* Street Beat when we hit the road.

The Spyderco Bushcraft has a thick, four-inch blade of 01 tool steel, a scandi grind, and a comfortable working handle. It's a bushcraft knife that's tougher than many purpose-designed survival knives. It cuts like the winter wind, is easy to sharpen and handy to carry. There's nothing not to like.

TOPS Knives

Tactical Operational Products
P.O. Box 2544
Idaho Falls, ID 83403
(208) 542–0113
www.topsknives.com

That's a TOPS Steel Eagle sticking in the side of an auto body. You might not ever need to cut your way out of a car, but most of TOPS knives have the strength, geometry, and properly heat-treated 1095 carbon steel to allow you to do so. The Steel Eagle is a war knife and not the best choice for a survival knife. One of the over one hundred models in the TOPS line could be. I particularly like the Mil Spec series. They'll do good woodwork and food prep as well as field dress autos.

Mike Fuller founded TOPS in 1998 with the idea of making a high-quality knife, not pretty, but highly functional and dependable. Mike told me he first saw this need "back in the day," as my young friends describe the sixties, "when a solider had to spend a month's pay to buy what we believed was the best knife available, a Randall." Although we did not meet at that time, Mike was at Smoke Bomb Hill about the same time that I was. His point of view on knives was formed in the same crucible as mine. As a special forces soldier, Mike went on to years of globe-girdling service with special forces and related civilian organizations. From Southeast Asia to Africa he served his country, expanded his experience, and refined his ideas about knives, about what works and what doesn't work. As a former SF solider who has spent more time in combat than the average politician has spent begging for money, Mike knows what he's doing. Here's the thing. Mike won't let you down. Neither will his knives. They are good to go.

Victorinox

Swiss Army Inc.
7 Victoria Drive
Monroe, CT 06468
www.swissarmy.com

Victorinox, the world-famous maker of Swiss Army Knives, now makes a number of models with locking blades, some of them with one-handed openers, thereby improving them for survival use. While appearing to be built too lightly for extreme use, the newer models are in the pockets of almost every survival instructor I know, which is about the best recommendation I can offer; besides the fact that I use them too. I have for years carried one of the models with a locking main blade, a wood saw (which actually works), the usual assortment of screwdrivers, and the most important tool of all, the tool that surpasses all other the tools, the essential tool: the corkscrew, without which many an evening would have been bereft of laughter and fun, and the bottled sunshine of the Rhone Valley would have remained in its bottle.

The fellow whom I wrote about earlier, who was taken by terrorists in Somalia and who used his SAK to escape, survived because he had one of these familiar, red-handled folders in his pocket. You might also.

Wayne Goddard Master Bladesmith

(541) 689–8098
www.goddardknives.com

Wayne Goddard's Camp Knife lives in my Go Bag. Wayne Goddard, Master Bladesmith, made this knife. Wayne forged and tempered the steel and formed the blade so that there is a full convex grind from spine to edge and a slight curve to the edge from hilt to tip. Everyone in my family, and all our friends who have worked with us doing survival skills, call it "Wayne's Knife." As in, "Can I use Wayne's Knife?" After trying it once, everyone wants to use Wayne's Knife.

I hesitate to tell you how well Wayne's knives perform. I've seen looks of disbelief from semi-knowledgeable knife people when I've talked about it in the past. In cutting tests and fieldwork, including knife-on-knife impact testing, this deceptively simple-looking knife has outperformed every blade that has been measured against it since I first got it in 1992. It weighs less than many four-inch tactical folders. The blade is only seven inches in length, yet it has outperformed both nine- and ten-inch choppers and four-inch slicers.

With proper technique, Wayne's Knife will slash though a three-inch standing sapling in one or two strokes. It slices meat like the best butcher knife and cuts through denim and heavy leather as if they were tissue paper. It will cut rope until your hand gets tired, which is a fairly long time since little effort is required. When the edge is tuned up, it will cut a falling silk scarf, a test that comes down to us from ancient times. It stays sharp for a looong time and is easy to sharpen when the time comes. I've bent the blade to thirty degrees and it sprang back to true with no deformation.

At one time I thought that this particular knife had to be a once-in-a-lifetime kind of thing. You know, when everything comes together just right: steel, heat treat, geometry, and the moon is in the right place. The seventh house or whatever. Then, at my request, Wayne made two more for me to give to my sons. My son's knives are slightly beefier than mine. They have a little more belly. But basically, they're the same knife.

If you are looking for absolute performance and if you don't mind waiting months to get a knife, you should give Wayne a call. I'm pretty sure there are other bladesmiths of the ABS capable of making knives that perform in the same range, but I haven't used their blades, and so cannot comment on them. I have used Wayne's Knife, and will continue to do so.

Yasen Nikov Knives

Kustendil 2500, str Iskar 11a
Bulgaria
nikovknives.com
yasen.nikov@gmail.com
FB: NikovKnives

▲ Fishing spear made with Yasen Nikov APK.

It's a good one, Yasen's knife. Classic clip-point design, good geometry, five inches of carbon steel with a full convex grind, proper heat treat, all the elements needed for a terrific blade. Combined with a comfortable G10 handle and a Kydex sheath that rides comfortably on your belt, it's a survival knife, field knife, utility knife, and a very good kitchen knife.

Over a period of two months, I batoned Yasen's knife through a stack of firewood, made a fire board and drill, a fish spear, and a rabbit stick. I cut up duck, beef, and pork, potatoes, carrots, tomatoes, cucumbers, and squash, sliced bread and cake. I also used it to cut up a stack of cardboard boxes and a pile of plastic bottles before taking them to the trash. It did everything well. It's an all-purpose knife, good for anything that needs cutting, I think of it as Yasen's APK.

With light batoning, the convex ground blade easily slipped through tough firewood that had been cured since last year. While splitting the shaft of a sapling to make a four-pointed fishing spear, the blade cut cleanly with full control, allowing me to separate the four points without breaking any of them. A scandi ground blade with which I was comparing it cracked a sapling from the same stand and spit it too deep, making the shaft unusable. Cutting the shafts was much easier with Yasen's knife than with the similar-sized scandi grind. Three quick snap cuts with the APK and I had a shaft to work with. The scandi ground blade required press cuts and whittling to get a shaft, much more work, much more time, which could matter in a survival situation. The convex ground allowed full control when planing the fire board and drilling holes for the drill.

Yasen's knife came hair-shaving sharp. Usually, I touch up a blade as needed to keep a prime edge at all times. As an experiment, I didn't touch Yasen's blade to stone, steel, or strop during the first three weeks I used it. At that time, after much batoning, woodwork, and so on, the blade still had a working edge. Stropping it on a leather strap with a little rouge brought it back to hair shaving sharp in about ten minutes.

Yasen makes good knives. Order direct from him and you won't be disappointed.

Zero Tolerance Knives

KAI USA
18600 SW Teton Avenue
Tualatin, OR 97062
(503) 682–1966
www.ztknives.com

▲ ZT Folder.

The ZT 0301 is not the knife with which to spread your Camembert at the wine tasting. It is to folding knives as the Abrams Tank is to the Toyota Prius. Hefty construction, a recurved blade, a bank-vault-solid lock, and a comfortable textured non-slip grip combine to make the ZT 0301 one of the toughest folders I've ever used, or seen. The ZT0350 is smaller, more pocketable version of the 0301. Both of them qualify as folding survival knives you can rely on.

ZT is well known for making top quality hard use folders. Two ZT models I especially like are the 0452CF and the 0462. Both designed by Dmitry Sinkevich, a knife maker who obviously knows what goes into a survival grade folder.

Sharpeners

DMT

Diamond Machining Technology
85 Hayes Memorial Drive
Marlborough, MA 01752 USA
(800) 666–4368
www.dmtsharp.com

EZE-LAP Diamond Sharpeners

www.eze-lap.com

Norton

All kinds of natural sharpening stones
www.nortonabrasives.com

Suggested Reading

Department of Defense. Map Reading and Land Navigation, *Department of the Army Field Manual No. 3-25-26*. This field manual is the standard. It has been used to train generations of service members. Free from the Department of the Army.

The U.S. Army Survival Manual, *Department of the Army Field Manual No. 21–76*. This field manual is a how-to of basic survival methods covering global conditions. It has been used effectively by generations of service members. Free from Department of the Army.

Hawke, Mykel. *Hawke's Special Forces Survival Handbook: The Portable Guide to Getting Out Alive*. Philadelphia: Running Press, 2011. Mykel Hawke is a retired special forces (Green Berets) captain and a certified special forces medic who has been deployed in hot spots around the world. I know Mykel, and he knows his topic. This book, based on real-world experience, differs on important points from the standard manual.

Lovelock, James. *A Rough Ride to the Future*. New York: Overlook Press, 2015. This book is by the scientist who developed the Gaia hypothesis, which is now accepted by scientists worldwide. A survival manual by a person with impeccable credentials.

Nessmuk [George W. Sears]. *Woodcraft & Camping*. Mineola, NY: Dover Publications, 1920. I first read this book at age ten. My mentor, Wabash Pete, could have written it. Many of these old-school methods are not appropriate for today's outdoorsmen; no longer can we down trees for a night's camping. But the spirit of the book, lightweight minimalism, is as valid today as ever.

Wescott, David, ed. *Primitive Technology: A Book of Earth Skills*. Layton, UT: Gibbs Smith, 1999. Dave Wescott was director of the Boulder Outdoor Survival School for many years and is a recognized authority on survival with primitive skills. I've trained with Dave and highly recommend this book if you're interested in this subject matter, and even if you're not.